Southern Living

FIX IT&
FREEZE IT
HEAT IT&
EAT IT

Oxmoor House®

©2012 by Time Home Entertainment Inc.
135 West 50th Street, New York, NY 10020

Southern Living® is a registered trademark of Time Inc. Lifestyle Group. All rights reserved. No part of this book may be reproduced in any form or by any means without the prior written permission of the publisher, excepting brief quotations in connection with reviews written specifically for inclusion in magazines or newspapers, or limited excerpts strictly for personal use.

ISBN-13: 978-0-8487-3649-1
ISBN-10: 0-8487-3649-4
Library of Congress Control Number: 2012942585

Printed in the United States of America
First Printing 2012

Oxmoor House
Editorial Director: Leah McLaughlin
Creative Director: Felicity Keane
Senior Brand Manager: Daniel Fagan
Senior Editor: Rebecca Brennan
Managing Editor: Rebecca Benton

Southern Living® Fix It & Freeze It, Heat It & Eat It
Editor: Susan Hernandez Ray
Project Editor: Megan McSwain Yeatts
Senior Designer: Melissa Clark
Director, Test Kitchen: Elizabeth Tyler Austin
Assistant Directors, Test Kitchen: Julie Christopher, Julie Gunter
Recipe Developers and Testers: Wendy Ball, R.D.;
    Victoria E. Cox; Stefanie Maloney; Callie Nash; Leah Van Deren
Recipe Editor: Alyson Moreland Haynes
Food Stylists: Margaret Monroe Dickey, Catherine Crowell Steele
Photography Director: Jim Bathie
Senior Photo Stylist: Kay E. Clarke
Photo Stylist: Katherine Eckert Coyne
Assistant Photo Stylist: Mary Louise Menendez
Production Manager: Theresa Beste-Farley

Contributors
Project Editor: Laura Hoxworth
Copy Editors: Donna Baldone, Barry Wise Smith
Proofreader: Mary Ann Laurens
Indexer: Mary Ann Laurens
Recipe Developers and Testers: Tamara Goldis, Erica Hopper, Tonya Johnson, Kyra Moncrief, Kathleen Royal Phillips
Photo Stylist: Anna Pollock
Interns: Morgan Bolling, Mackenzie Cogle, Susan Kemp, Alicia Lavender, Anna Pollock, Emily Robinson, Ashley White

Southern Living®
Editor: M. Lindsay Bierman
Creative Director: Robert Perino
Managing Editor: Candace Higginbotham
Art Director: Chris Hoke
Associate Art Director: Erynn Hassinger
Executive Editors: Rachel Hardage Barrett, Jessica S. Thuston
Food Director: Shannon Sliter Satterwhite
Test Kitchen Director: Rebecca Kracke Gordon
Senior Writer: Donna Florio
Senior Food Editor: Mary Allen Perry
Assistant Recipe Editor: Ashley Arthur
Test Kitchen Professionals: Norman King, Pam Lolley, Angela Sellers
Test Kitchen Specialist/Food Styling: Vanessa McNeil Rocchio
Recipe Editor: JoAnn Weatherly
Foods Copy Editor: Ashley Leath
Senior Photographers: Ralph Lee Anderson, Gary Clark, Art Meripol
Photographers: Robbie Caponetto, Laurey W. Glenn
Photo Research Coordinator: Ginny P. Allen
Senior Photo Stylist: Buffy Hargett
Editorial Assistant: Pat York

Time Home Entertainment Inc.
Publisher: Jim Childs
VP, Strategy & Business Development: Steven Sandonato
Executive Director, Marketing Services: Carol Pittard
Executive Director, Retail & Special Sales: Tom Mifsud
Director, Bookazine Development & Marketing: Laura Adam
Executive Publishing Director: Joy Butts
Finance Director: Glenn Buonocore
Associate General Counsel: Helen Wan

To order additional publications, call
1-800-765-6400 or 1-800-491-0551.

For more books to enrich your life, visit **oxmoorhouse.com**

To search, savor, and share thousands
of recipes, visit **myrecipes.com**

Cover:
Orange-Ginger Glazed Carrots, page 211;
Penne Casserole, page 227;
Okra-and-Corn Maque Choux, page 97

Back Cover:
Pork Fajitas, page 49;
Strawberry-Orange Pops, page 248

CONTENTS

WELCOME

The last thing you want to worry about after a hectic day is the hassle and stress of exhausting dinner prep. Luckily, by taking an organized approach, you can get a head start and avoid the usual dinnertime dilemma with make-ahead meals that will bring happiness to the supper table.

Forget the drive-thru and feed your family wholesome dishes straight from the oven. Get a jump start on your evening meal with sauces, marinades, pie crusts, and more. Freeze ahead the tasty Marinara Sauce (page 21) to make headway on the Italian Meatballs (page 235). Or, keep your freezer stocked with pizza dough (page 28) so that you can prepare a quick homemade pizza any night of the week.

Our Double Duty chapter shows you how to save time and money by making the most of main ingredients. Buy in bulk and use a portion of lean ground beef to make Meaty Spaghetti Sauce (page 36). You can freeze leftovers up to three months and use later to make Stuffed Shells Florentine (page 37).

Bring everyone to the table with our collection of more than 200 test kitchen-approved recipes. We've included family-friendly dishes like Chicken Enchiladas (page 113) and Make-Ahead Beefy Lasagna (page 80). With crowd favorites like Spicy White Cheese Dip (page 126) and Golden-Baked Mini Reubens (page 142), you can toss your next party at a moment's notice.

And don't forget dessert! Our Do-Ahead Desserts (page 251) make satisfying your sweet tooth a cinch. Mint Chocolate Chip Ice-Cream Cake (page 267) is a mint-lover's dream and can be made up to a month in advance. Our White Chocolate-Covered Pretzel Cookies (page 299) are the perfect balance of salty and sweet and will keep in the freezer up to three months.

Whether you're looking for go-to meals to serve your family or party-ready foods to impress your guests, you'll find everything you need to fix, freeze, heat, and eat.

From my freezer to yours,

Susan

Susan Ray
Editor

Forget the drive-thru and feed your family wholesome dishes straight from the oven. Get a jump start on your evening meal with sauces, marinades, pie crusts, and more.

plan ahead to
make ahead

HOW TO PROPERLY FREEZE FOODS

Preparing double or even triple recipes and freezing portions for later means you don't have to cook every night to have a delicious and nutritious meal on the table.

Freshness and quality of the food at the time of freezing affect the condition of frozen foods. If foods are frozen at the peak of their quality, they emerge tasting better than foods frozen near the end of their freshness. So freeze items you won't use in the near future sooner rather than later. It's important to store all foods at 0° or lower in order to retain vitamin content, color, flavor, and texture.

FREEZE SMART Some food is better suited to freezing and reheating than others. Casseroles, soups, stews, chili, and meatloaf all freeze well. See a more precise list beginning on page 12.

COOL OFF To keep food safe, cool freshly cooked dishes quickly before freezing. Putting foods that are still warm in the freezer can raise the temperature, causing surrounding frozen items to partially thaw and refreeze, which can alter the taste and texture of some foods. Place food in a shallow, wide container and refrigerate, uncovered, until cool. To chill soup or stew even faster, pour it into a metal bowl and set in an ice bath—a larger bowl filled halfway with ice water. Stir occasionally.

For stews, braises, or other semiliquid dishes with some fat content, chill completely, and then skim the fat from the top before freezing. Fat spoils over time in the freezer and shortens a dish's frozen shelf life.

CHOOSE THE RIGHT CONTAINER Check the directions on zip-top plastic freezer bags and wrapping materials for guidelines on microwave use. They may be recommended for defrosting foods but not for reheating at a higher level of power. Make sure you use containers designed for the freezer. Flimsy sandwich bags will not withstand time in the freezer, and even glass can sometimes crack as food expands in the freezer.

PROTECT YOUR FOOD Avoid freezer burn by using moisture-proof zip-top plastic freezer bags and wrap. Remove the air from bags before sealing. Store soups and stews in freezer bags, which can be placed flat and freeze quickly. Store foods in small servings, no more than 1 quart, so they freeze quickly. This also allows you to defrost only what you need. Use a permanent marker to label each container with the name of the dish, volume or weight if you've measured it, and the date you put it in the freezer. Also include baking or reheating instructions. It's easier to write on plastic freezer bags before you freeze them.

CONTROL PORTIONS Whenever possible, freeze in smaller batches since they tend to freeze faster than larger batches and will taste better when thawed.

DON'T OVERCROWD The quicker food freezes, the better its quality once thawed. Do not crowd the freezer—arrange containers in a single layer in the freezer to allow enough room for air to circulate around them so food will freeze rapidly. Slowly frozen food forms large ice crystals that may turn the food mushy. Most cooked dishes will keep for two to three months in the freezer. Use a freezer thermometer to ensure that your unit remains at 0° or below. Always cool food to room temperature before freezing.

GET ORGANIZED If your freezer doesn't have any built-in organizational features, create your own by purchasing inexpensive plastic storage containers to group like foods together. Label bins to make finding what you need even easier. If there isn't a rack, add plastic-coated, free-standing wire shelves to increase the storage space.

shortcut secret

Shop one day; then prepare meals for the freezer the next. This will make your to-do list for each day manageable. Chop any vegetables you'll need for your recipes, such as onions, mushrooms, and peppers, and line them up on your counter for easy assembly. Then move on to the meat preparation.

WHAT TO FREEZE

Casseroles

Everyone loves a good casserole, and this little trick lets you stock the freezer without tying up your dishes.

Line the bottom and sides of a casserole dish with heavy-duty aluminum foil, allowing 2 to 3 inches to extend over sides; fill with prepared recipe.
Cover and freeze two to three hours or until firm.
Lift the frozen casserole from the dish, using the foil sides as handles, and freeze in a labeled zip-top plastic freezer bag. You'll need an extra-large 2-gallon bag for 13- x 9-inch baking dishes, and a 1-gallon bag for 9-inch square baking dishes.
To serve, remove the foil from frozen casserole, and return casserole to original baking dish; cover and let thaw in the refrigerator (allow 24 to 48 hours). Let stand 30 minutes at room temperature, and bake as directed.

Soups and Stews

Cool the soup by placing the pot of soup in a bath of ice water in the sink. Stir soup often to help release the heat. Package and date quart- or gallon-size zip-top plastic freezer bags, place in a bowl, and cuff the bag over the edge. Ladle soup into each bag, then let out any excess air and seal.

TO FREEZE IT: lay bags flat in a single layer in the freezer; when frozen, stack bags to save space.

Baked Goods

To quick-freeze individual cupcakes, tarts, and other baked goods, arrange in a single layer in a jelly-roll pan, and freeze one to two hours or until firm. Transfer to an airtight container or zip-top plastic freezer bag, and remove desired portions as needed. Many savory items, such as meatballs or twice-baked potatoes, can be frozen in the same way.
To prevent wrapping from sticking to frosting, quick-freeze cakes, uncovered, until firm, and then package.
To serve, remove wrapping, and thaw overnight in the refrigerator in a protective container or cake keeper.

Cookies

For a batch of fresh-baked cookies any time, store cookie dough in the freezer up to six months.

TO FREEZE IT: shape cookie dough into logs, and wrap in parchment paper. To prevent flattening on one side, place each log inside an empty cardboard tube from gift wrap or paper towels. Place in zip-top plastic freezer bags.

Or, shape dough with a small ice cream scoop; lightly roll dough between palms to create smooth balls. Place on a baking sheet, freeze until firm, and transfer to a zip-top plastic freezer bag. Allow 2 to 3 extra minutes baking time for frozen dough.

Another option is to pack dough in an airtight container or zip-top plastic freezer bag. Before baking, thaw frozen dough in the refrigerator overnight.

Seasonal Berries

Take advantage of the luscious blueberries, raspberries, and blackberries available in the summer. Buy extra, and freeze them for summer-fresh flavor year-round. Frozen berries make great additions to smoothies, pancakes, muffins, pies, and cobblers.

TO FREEZE IT: sort berries, discarding any mushy, underripe, or damaged ones. Gently rinse in cool water. (Do not rinse blueberries.) Pat dry with a paper towel. Place berries in a single layer on a jelly-roll pan; freeze until firm. Transfer berries to a labeled and dated zip-top plastic freezer bag, squeezing out excess air. Freeze up to nine months. Add berries to your favorite recipes while still frozen. Briefly rinse frozen blueberries with cool water just before using.

JUMP-START INGREDIENTS

Stock your freezer with cooked ground meats, cubed chicken or turkey, and shredded cheese, and you can assemble family-pleasing main dishes in a snap.

• Pint- to gallon-size zip-top plastic freezer bags are excellent choices for storing food items. (A pint-size zip-top plastic freezer bag is perfect for 1 cup cubed cooked chicken breasts.) Also check out the great plastic freezer container choices that go from freezer to microwave to dishwasher. They come in several sizes, including 3 cups. Whichever you choose, make sure you purchase good-quality bags and containers that are designed for the freezer.

• Label your items for freezing, including the amount and date. If properly stored, shredded cheeses and cooked meats can be frozen up to three months.

• 1 to 1¼ lb. uncooked lean ground beef, turkey, or sausage = about 2½ to 3 cups cooked and crumbled

• 1¼ to 1½ lb. uncooked chicken breasts = about 3 cups cooked and cubed

• Preshredded cheeses are convenient and freeze well but can be costly. Consider grating your own (2 [8-oz.] blocks of cheese, shredded = about 4 cups). Partially freezing the block, especially softer cheeses such as Swiss and Monterey Jack, makes grating a breeze.

• Chopped onions show up as an ingredient in lots of recipes. You can freeze them after chopping, but freeze them raw.

How Long Will It Keep?

Save money by buying in bulk or stocking up with supermarket specials, then freeze the items that you won't be using right away. Wrap completely cooled food in heavy-duty plastic wrap or aluminum foil, and place in zip-top plastic freezer bags or airtight containers to preserve the texture and flavor. Here's our guide to how long you can store a variety of foods in the freezer and maintain quality.

Meats

Bacon, raw = 1 month
Sausage, raw = 1–2 months
Ham, fully cooked = 1–2 months
Luncheon meats, unopened = 1–2 months
Cooked meats, casseroles = 2–3 months
Cooked soups/stews = 2–3 months
Ground beef, veal, lamb, pork = 3–4 months
Chops = 4 months
Roasts = 4 months
Steaks = 6 months

Dairy

Yogurt = 1–2 months
Ice Cream = 2 months
Milk = 1 month
Cream, half-and-half = 4 months
Cheese, hard, unopened = 6 months
Cheese, soft, unopened = 6 months
Butter = 6–9 months

Poultry

Ground chicken, turkey = 3–4 months
Cooked, plain = 4 months
Cooked poultry, casseroles = 4–6 months
Cooked, covered with broth, gravy = 6 months
Chicken or turkey, pieces = 9 months
Chicken or turkey, whole = 12 months

Fruit and Vegetables

Vegetables, purchased frozen = 8 months
Juices, unopened = 8–12 months
Fruit juice concentrates = 12 months
Vegetables, home-frozen = 10 months

Fish and Shellfish

Fish, fatty = 2–3 months
Live clams, crab, lobster, mussels,
     oysters = 2–3 months
Shellfish, cooked = 3 months
Shrimp, scallops, shucked clams, mussels,
     oysters = 3–6 months
Fish, cooked = 4–6 months
Fish, lean = 6 months

Breads and Desserts

Pie, baked = 1 month
Cake, angel food, chiffon, sponge = 2 months
Cheesecake = 1–2 months
Quick bread, baked = 2–3 months
Yeast bread and rolls = 3–6 months
Cake, yellow or pound = 1–3 months
Cookies, baked = 1–3 months

jump starts

MARINADES & RUBS

- For variety, make several different recipes of marinades and rubs.
- Prick chicken several times with a fork to allow flavors to penetrate the meat.
- Combine marinade and chicken breasts in labeled zip-top plastic freezer bags.
- Seal bags, and gently knead the meat to circulate the marinade. Lay bags flat with meat side by side in a flat pan with sides.
- Marinate for desired time in refrigerator.

TO FREEZE IT: Place pan in freezer; freeze bags flat. To reheat, remove frozen bags from pan, and stack in freezer. Thaw in fridge. For kabobs or stir-fry, cut chicken breasts into cubes or strips, and follow the same instructions.

Pair each marinade with its specific recipe, or use on skinned and boned chicken breasts before baking, grilling, or stir-frying.

Use this marinade with the Zesty Chicken Kabobs on page 244.

ZESTY CHICKEN MARINADE

Makes: about ½ cup   Hands-on Time: 10 min.   Total Time: 10 min.

4 garlic cloves, minced	1 tsp. ground cumin
1 small onion, finely chopped	1 tsp. dried parsley flakes
⅓ cup chopped fresh cilantro	½ tsp. salt
¼ cup olive oil	½ tsp. ground red pepper
1½ tsp. paprika	

1. Combine all ingredients. Store in a labeled container in refrigerator.

Use this rub with the Mediterranean Steak on page 226.

MEDITERRANEAN RUB

Makes: about ½ cup   Hands-on Time: 10 min.   Total Time: 10 min.

2 tsp. ground sage	1 tsp. salt
2 tsp. dried thyme	1 tsp. garlic powder
2 tsp. pepper	1 tsp. dried rosemary, crushed

1. Combine all ingredients. Store in a labeled airtight container. Use for lamb, chicken, or beef.

Use this marinade with the Italian Steak on page 226.

ITALIAN MARINADE

Makes: 1¼ cups   Hands-on Time: 10 min.   Total Time: 10 min.

1 cup olive oil	1 Tbsp. chopped fresh rosemary
¼ cup red wine vinegar	1 Tbsp. soy sauce
3 shallots, peeled and chopped	2 tsp. pepper
6 garlic cloves, chopped	

1. Combine all ingredients. Store in a labeled container in refrigerator. Use to marinate poultry, beef, or lamb.

Rub spice blend over 6 skinned and boned chicken breast halves. Grill, covered with grill lid, over medium-high heat (350° to 400°) for 6 to 7 minutes on each side or until done.

SOUTHWESTERN SPICE BLEND

Makes: ¼ cup   Hands-on Time: 5 min.   Total Time: 5 min.

1 Tbsp. salt	2 tsp. ground cumin
2 tsp. garlic powder	2 tsp. pepper
2 tsp. chili powder	½ tsp. unsweetened cocoa

1. Combine all ingredients. Store in a labeled airtight container. Use as a meat or poultry rub or to flavor chili and soups.

Keep this sauce on hand to use with Sausage-and-Cheese Calzone, page 93; Parmesan Twists, page 147; and Pepperoni Pizza, page 232.

ZESTY PIZZA SAUCE

Makes: 3 cups   Hands-on Time: 20 min.   Total Time: 1 hr., 35 min.

1 large onion, chopped	1 Tbsp. dried Italian seasoning
4 garlic cloves, minced	¾ tsp. salt
2 Tbsp. olive oil	½ tsp. pepper
1 (28-oz.) can diced tomatoes	¼ tsp. dried crushed red pepper

1. Sauté onion and garlic in hot olive oil in a 3-qt. saucepan over medium-high heat 10 minutes or until tender. Stir tomatoes, Italian seasoning, salt, pepper, and crushed red pepper into onion mixture. Bring to a boil; reduce heat to low, and simmer, stirring occasionally, 1 hour. Let stand 15 minutes. Process tomato mixture in a blender or food processor, in batches, until smooth. Cover and chill up to 5 days. Reheat in a saucepan over medium-low heat.

TO FREEZE IT: Cool quickly. Divide sauce into 2 labeled zip-top plastic freezer bags or containers, leaving room at the top. Freeze up to 4 months. Thaw in fridge overnight. Reheat in a saucepan over medium-low heat.

Store this barbecue sauce in the freezer for quick weeknight suppers or for dippers with recipes such as the Oven-Fried Parmesan Chicken Strips on page 240.

HONEY-BARBECUE SAUCE

Makes: 2¾ cups   Hands-on Time: 30 min.   Total Time: 30 min.

2 cups ketchup	2 Tbsp. white vinegar
1 cup dry white wine	2 Tbsp. lemon juice
⅓ cup honey	1 Tbsp. Worcestershire sauce
1 small onion, diced	1 tsp. hot sauce
2 garlic cloves, minced	¼ tsp. salt
1 Tbsp. dried parsley flakes	

1. Bring all ingredients to a boil in a large saucepan; reduce heat, and simmer, stirring often, 15 to 20 minutes or until slightly thickened.

TO FREEZE IT: Cool 15 minutes. Place mixture in a labeled zip-top plastic freezer bag; freeze up to 4 months. Thaw in fridge. Reheat in a saucepan over medium-low heat before serving.

Make this sauce ahead to use with the Italian Meatballs on page 235 or as a marinara in your other favorite recipes.

MARINARA SAUCE

Makes: about 6 cups   Hands-on Time: 15 min.   Total Time: 15 min.

1   cup beef broth
½   cup dry red wine
1   (26-oz.) jar marinara sauce

1   (8-oz.) can tomato sauce with basil, garlic, and oregano

1. Stir together beef broth, wine, ½ cup water, marinara sauce, and tomato sauce. Cook over medium heat, stirring occasionally, 10 minutes or until thoroughly heated.

TO FREEZE IT: Cool 15 minutes. Divide sauce into 2 labeled zip-top plastic freezer bags. Freeze up to 4 months. Thaw in fridge overnight. Reheat in a saucepan over medium heat.

SAVORY MEAT BASE

Makes: 8 cups   Hands-on Time: 30 min.   Total Time: 40 min.

3   lb. lean ground beef
2   large onions, chopped
1   large green bell pepper, chopped

1   tsp. bottled minced garlic
1   (26-oz.) jar marinara sauce
1   tsp. salt
½   tsp. pepper

1. Cook first 4 ingredients in a large Dutch oven over medium-high heat; stir until meat is crumbled and no longer pink. Drain mixture; return to Dutch oven.
2. Stir in marinara sauce, salt, and pepper; cover and simmer, stirring occasionally, 15 minutes. Cool 10 minutes.

TO FREEZE IT: Divide mixture into 2 labeled zip-top plastic freezer bags; freeze up to 4 months. Thaw in fridge overnight. Reheat in a saucepan over medium heat.

Note: Keep this recipe starter in the freezer to make a delicious spaghetti with meat sauce. Heat 4 cups of Savory Meat Base, thawed, in a Dutch oven over medium heat. Stir in 1 (14½-oz.) can diced tomatoes with Italian herbs, 1 (8-oz.) can tomato sauce, 1 tsp. dried Italian seasoning, and ½ tsp. dried basil. Cover, reduce heat, and simmer 20 minutes. Serve over 12 ounces hot cooked spaghetti with a tossed green salad and garlic bread. Makes: 6 servings.

Try using this zesty mixture as a tasty substitute for pizza sauce.

SUN-DRIED TOMATO PESTO

Makes: 1½ cups   Hands-on Time: 10 min.   Total Time: 10 min.

2 (3-oz.) packages sun-dried tomato halves	½ cup olive oil
½ cup grated Parmesan cheese	¼ cup pine nuts
½ cup loosely packed fresh flat-leaf parsley	3 garlic cloves
	3 Tbsp. cold water
	1 Tbsp. lemon juice

1. Process all ingredients in a food processor until smooth, stopping to scrape down sides as needed.

TO FREEZE IT: Transfer to a labeled quart-size zip-top plastic freezer bag; seal. Lay bag flat in freezer. Thaw in fridge overnight.

Stir a spoonful or two of Herb Pesto into lightly beaten eggs to make a seasoned omelet or scrambled eggs.

HERB PESTO

Makes: 1 cup   Hands-on Time: 10 min.   Total Time: 10 min.

⅔ cup olive oil	¼ cup cold water
½ cup loosely packed fresh basil leaves	1 to 2 garlic cloves
½ cup loosely packed fresh flat-leaf parsley leaves	2 Tbsp. fresh oregano leaves
	1 Tbsp. fresh rosemary leaves
½ cup grated Parmesan cheese	1 Tbsp. lemon juice
¼ cup pine nuts	½ tsp. salt
	½ tsp. pepper

1. Process all ingredients in a food processor until smooth, stopping to scrape down sides as needed.

TO FREEZE IT: Transfer to a labeled quart-size zip-top plastic freezer bag; seal. Lay bag flat in freezer. Thaw in fridge overnight.

Spread this over grilled corn, or toss with chopped grilled veggies for extra flavor.

CILANTRO PESTO

Makes: 2 cups   Hands-on Time: 15 min.   Total Time: 35 min.

- ½ cup chopped pecans
- 1 tsp. cumin seeds
- 2 cups loosely packed fresh cilantro leaves
- ½ cup grated Parmesan cheese
- ⅓ cup olive oil
- ¼ cup cold water
- 2 garlic cloves
- 1 Tbsp. lemon juice
- ½ tsp. salt

1. Preheat oven to 350°. Bake pecans in a single layer in a shallow pan 5 to 6 minutes or until toasted and fragrant, stirring halfway through. Cool 10 minutes.

2. Meanwhile, place a small skillet over medium-high heat until hot; add cumin seeds, and cook, stirring constantly, 1 to 2 minutes or until toasted. Cool 10 minutes.

3. Process pecans, cumin seeds, and next 7 ingredients in a food processor until smooth, stopping to scrape down sides as needed.

TO FREEZE IT: Transfer to a labeled quart-size zip-top plastic freezer bag; seal. Lay bag flat in freezer. Thaw in fridge overnight.

Spoon this over goat cheese or warm Brie for an easy party appetizer.

OLIVE PESTO

Makes: about 2 cups   Hands-on Time: 10 min.   Total Time: 10 min.

- 1 (7-oz.) jar pitted kalamata olives, drained
- 1 (7-oz.) jar pimiento-stuffed Spanish olives, drained
- ¼ cup grated Parmesan cheese
- 3 Tbsp. olive oil
- 2 Tbsp. balsamic vinegar
- 3 to 4 garlic cloves
- 1 tsp. pepper
- 1 tsp. smoked paprika

1. Process all ingredients in a food processor until smooth, stopping to scrape down sides as needed.

TO FREEZE IT: Transfer to a labeled quart-size zip-top plastic freezer bag; seal. Lay bag flat in freezer. Thaw in fridge overnight.

Use this in the French Onion Soup on page 64.

CARAMELIZED ONIONS

Makes: 2 cups   Hands-on Time: 10 min.   Total Time: 8 hr., 10 min.

2   extra-large sweet onions
    (about 3 lb.)

1   (10½-oz.) can beef consommé
¼   cup butter

1. Cut onions in half; cut each half into ½-inch-thick slices. Combine all ingredients in a 3½-qt. slow cooker. Cover and cook on HIGH 8 hours or until golden brown and very soft. Store onions in an airtight container; refrigerate up to 2 weeks.

TO FREEZE IT: Transfer onions to a quart-size labeled zip-top plastic freezer bag; seal. Lay bag flat in freezer. Freeze up to 2 months. Thaw in fridge overnight.

MAKE-AHEAD TURKEY GRAVY

Makes: 4 cups   Hands-on Time: 37 min.   Total Time: 1 hr., 52 min.

2¼ lb. turkey drumsticks
3   carrots, cut into pieces
1   large onion, quartered
6   fresh parsley sprigs
⅓   cup vegetable oil

½   cup all-purpose flour
6   cups low-sodium fat-free
    chicken broth
½   tsp. pepper
Salt to taste

1. Preheat oven to 400°. Pat drumsticks dry. Cook drumsticks and next 3 ingredients in hot oil in a large roasting pan over medium-high heat. Cook drumsticks 3 minutes on each side; cook vegetables, at the same time, stirring often.

2. Bake drumsticks and vegetables in pan at 400° for 30 minutes or until a meat thermometer inserted into thickest portion of drumsticks registers 165°. Remove from oven. Remove and discard vegetables and parsley using a slotted spoon. Reserve drumsticks for another use.

3. Whisk flour into hot drippings in pan, and cook over medium heat, whisking constantly, 1 minute. Gradually whisk in chicken broth until smooth. Whisk in pepper.

4. Bring to a boil over medium-high heat, whisking occasionally. Reduce heat to medium, and gently boil, whisking occasionally, 45 minutes or until thick enough to coat the back of a spoon. Season with salt to taste.

TO FREEZE IT: Divide mixture into 2 labeled zip-top plastic freezer bags; freeze up to 2 months. Thaw in fridge overnight.

JALAPEÑO-CRANBERRY CHUTNEY

Makes: 3 cups   Hands-on Time: 20 min.   Total Time: 20 min.

1   (12-oz.) package fresh cranberries
1   medium tangerine, cut into 8 wedges and seeded
½   cup red wine vinegar
¼   cup chopped shallots (2 large)
½   cup sugar
¼   cup minced seeded jalapeño pepper (3 peppers)
¼   tsp. salt
¼   tsp. black pepper

1. Place cranberries and tangerine wedges in a food processor; process until coarsely chopped, stopping to scrape down sides.

2. Bring vinegar and shallots to a boil in a saucepan. Reduce heat, and simmer, uncovered, 5 minutes or until mixture is reduced to ⅓ cup. Stir in cranberry mixture, sugar, and remaining ingredients. Cook over medium-low heat 5 minutes, stirring frequently. Serve chutney warm or chilled.

TO FREEZE IT: Transfer chutney to a labeled quart-size zip-top plastic freezer bag; seal. Lay bag flat in freezer. Thaw in fridge overnight.

SWEET TOMATO CHUTNEY

Makes: 1 cup   Hands-on Time: 10 min.   Total Time: 30 min.

½   sweet onion, finely chopped
1   garlic clove, minced
1   Tbsp. olive oil
1   (14.5-oz.) can diced tomatoes
3   Tbsp. light brown sugar
1   Tbsp. finely grated fresh ginger
1   Tbsp. fresh lime juice
2   tsp. apple cider vinegar
¼   tsp. salt
¼   tsp. dried crushed red pepper
1   mango, peeled and finely diced
1   Tbsp. finely chopped fresh cilantro

1. Sauté onion and garlic in hot oil in a medium saucepan over medium heat 4 minutes or until onion is tender. Add tomatoes and next 6 ingredients. Cook, stirring occasionally, 10 minutes or until almost all liquid evaporates. Stir in mango, and cook 1 minute. Let cool 20 minutes. Stir in cilantro. Serve warm, or cover and chill until ready to serve.

TO FREEZE IT: Transfer chutney to a labeled quart-size zip-top plastic freezer bag; seal. Lay bag flat in freezer. Thaw in fridge overnight.

Freeze these tasty butters ahead of time to use with biscuits. Also try them with the Simple Sweet Potato Biscuits on page 151.

CINNAMON-HONEY BUTTER

Makes: ½ cup   Hands-on Time: 10 min.   Total Time: 10 min.

½ cup unsalted butter, softened   1 tsp. ground cinnamon
2 Tbsp. honey

1. Beat butter at medium speed with an electric mixer until light and fluffy. Add honey and cinnamon, beating until well blended. Place butter on wax paper, and shape into 1 (5-inch) log.

Orange Butter: Add ¼ cup sifted powdered sugar and 1 Tbsp. orange zest to beaten butter, beating well. Serve with biscuits and pancakes. Makes: ½ cup.

Chive Butter: Add ¼ cup minced fresh chives to beaten butter, beating well. Serve with broiled chicken, fish, pasta, or potatoes. Makes: ½ cup.

Garlic Butter: Add 2 Tbsp. minced fresh parsley and 1 Tbsp. crushed garlic to beaten butter, beating well. Serve with bread, broiled seafood, or cooked vegetables. Makes: ½ cup.

TO FREEZE IT: Cover tightly, label, and freeze up to 6 months. Thaw in fridge or at room temperature to soften.

Preserve strawberries with this delicious recipe.
Pair it with Hurry-Up Homemade Crescent Rolls
on page 148 or your favorite biscuits or scones.

FROZEN STRAWBERRY FREEZER JAM

Makes: about 5 cups   Hands-on Time: 15 min.   Total Time: 5 hr.

6 cups frozen strawberries	1 (1.59-oz.) envelope freezer jam pectin
1½ cups sugar	

1. Place frozen strawberries in refrigerator 4 hours or until partially thawed. (Some ice crystals should be visible.)

2. Pulse strawberries in a food processor 8 to 12 times or until slightly chunky, stopping to scrape down sides. Place mixture in a medium bowl; stir in sugar, and let stand 15 minutes.

3. Gradually stir in pectin. Stir for 3 minutes, and let stand 30 minutes.

TO FREEZE IT: Spoon fruit mixture into 5 labeled 8-ounce sterilized canning jars, filling to ½ inch from top; wipe jar rims. Cover at once with metal lids, and screw on bands. Place in freezer. Thaw in fridge.

Note: We tested with Ball freezer jars.

DOUBLE BERRY FREEZER JAM

Makes: about 5 cups   Hands-on Time: 10 min.   Total Time: 30 min.

4 cups fresh blueberries	1 (1.59-oz.) envelope freezer jam pectin
3 cups fresh strawberries	
1½ cups sugar	

1. Pulse blueberries in food processor 2 to 4 times or until finely chopped, stopping to scrape down sides. Place in a medium-size bowl. Pulse strawberries in food processor 8 to 10 times or until finely chopped, stopping to scrape down sides. Add to blueberries in bowl. Stir in sugar, and let stand 15 minutes.

2. Gradually stir in pectin. Stir for 3 minutes; let stand 5 minutes.

TO FREEZE IT: Spoon mixture into 5 labeled 8-ounce sterilized canning jars, filling to ½ inch from top; wipe jar rims. Cover at once with metal lids, and screw on bands. Place in freezer. Thaw in fridge.

PIZZA DOUGH

Makes: 3 (8 oz.) portions   Hands-on Time: 15 min.   Total Time: 1 hr., 50 min.

2	cups warm water (100° to 110°)	6	to 7 cups all-purpose flour, divided
¼	tsp. sugar	1	Tbsp. salt
2	(¼-oz.) envelopes active dry yeast	2	Tbsp. extra virgin olive oil
			Vegetable cooking spray

1. Stir together warm water and sugar in a 2-cup measuring cup. Sprinkle with yeast, and let stand 5 to 7 minutes or until mixture is bubbly.

2. Place 6 cups flour and salt in food processor bowl. With motor running, add yeast mixture and olive oil; process mixture until dough forms. (If dough is too sticky, add more flour, 2 Tbsp. at a time.) Place dough in a large bowl coated with cooking spray; lightly coat dough with cooking spray. Cover with a clean cloth, and let rise in a warm place (85°), free from drafts, 1 hour or until doubled in bulk.

3. Punch dough down. Turn dough in bowl, and coat with cooking spray; cover with cloth, and let rise in a warm place 30 minutes or until doubled in bulk.

TO FREEZE IT: Cut dough into 12 equal portions, shaping each portion into a 3-inch ball immediately, or wrap in wax paper, place in a labeled zip-top plastic freezer bag, and freeze up to 1 month. Thaw in fridge overnight.

Try this pizza dough with the Pepperoni Pizza on page 232. Keep dough on hand for family pizza night.

PASTRY SHELL

Makes: 1 (9-inch) pastry shell   Hands-on Time: 15 min.   Total Time: 15 min.

- 2   cups all-purpose flour
- ¼   tsp. salt
- 3   Tbsp. shortening
- 2   Tbsp. cold butter
- 2   to 3 Tbsp. cold water

1. Combine flour and salt; cut in shortening and butter with a pastry blender until mixture resembles coarse meal. Sprinkle cold water (1 Tbsp. at a time) over surface; stir with a fork until dry ingredients are moistened. Shape pastry into a ball; chill.

2. Roll pastry to ⅛-inch thickness on a lightly floured surface. Place in a 9-inch pie plate or tart pan; trim excess pastry along edges.

TO FREEZE IT: Cover tightly, and freeze up to 6 months. To bake pastry shell, thaw slightly, and prick bottom and sides of pastry shell generously with a fork. Bake at 450° for 12 to 14 minutes or until pastry shell is golden brown. For filled pies, thaw pastry shell, and follow directions in specific recipes.

CHOCOLATE CRUMB CRUST

Makes: 1 (9-inch) crust   Hands-on Time: 15 min.   Total Time: 23 min.

- 1½ cups chocolate wafer crumbs
- ⅓   cup butter, melted

1. Preheat oven to 350°. Combine crumbs and butter in a small bowl; stir well. Firmly press crumb mixture on bottom and up sides of a 9-inch pie plate. Bake at 350° for 8 minutes. Cool completely.

TO FREEZE IT: Cover tightly, label, and freeze up to 6 months.

Freeze this crust ahead to use for your next pie. You can also substitute it for the ready-made crusts in the Chocolate Icebox Pie on page 276 or the Mocha-Pecan Mud Pie on page 277.

Use these pastries with the Tiny Caramel Tarts on page 289.

CREAM CHEESE PASTRY SHELLS

Makes: 6 dozen   Hands-on Time: 10 min.   Total Time: 1 hr., 35 min.

1   cup butter, softened
1   (8-oz.) package cream
    cheese, softened

3½ cups all-purpose flour

1. Beat butter and cream cheese at medium speed with a heavy-duty electric stand mixer until creamy. Gradually add flour to butter mixture, beating at low speed just until blended. Shape dough into 72 (¾-inch) balls, and place on a baking sheet; cover and chill 1 hour.

2. Preheat oven to 400°. Place dough balls in cups of lightly greased miniature muffin pans; press dough to top of cups, forming shells.

3. Bake at 400° for 10 to 12 minutes. Remove from pans to wire racks, and cool completely (about 15 minutes).

TO FREEZE IT: Baked pastry shells may be made up to 1 month ahead and frozen in a labeled airtight container. Thaw at room temperature before filling.

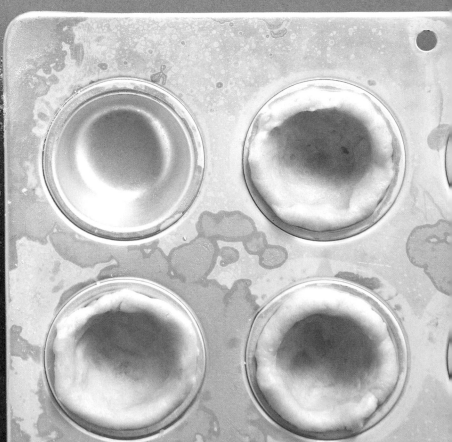

y spaghetti sauce }
What's in the bag?

Easy Barbecued chicken }
What's in the bag?

JAN ·	JULY	1 12 13 14 15 16
FEB	AUG	17 18 19 10 11 12
MAR	SEPT	13 (14) 15 16 17 18
APR	OCT	19 20 21 22 23 24
MAY	NOV	25 26 27 28 29 30
JUNE	DEC	31

Note: use in hearty brunswick stew

double duty

Recipe

TITLE: loaded cuban sandwiches
NOTES:
use margarita grilled pork tenderloin   PREP TIME:
                                              TOTAL TIME: 7 min
INGREDIENTS:
• 4 hoagie rolls   • 1/4 lb thinly sliced deli
• 1/4 cup dijon mustard   ham
• 1 margarita grilled pork   • 8 dill pickle slices
                                    • 8 swiss cheese slices

PICADILLO

Makes: 8 servings **plus 2⅔ cups for Picadillo-Stuffed Peppers**
Hands-on Time: 20 min.   Total Time: 27 min.

Picadillo remains a popular dish because it's so easy to make and because of its appealing flavors. Other renditions of picadillo include cinnamon and cloves, but this is the traditional Cuban version.

1 cup chopped onion	¼ cup golden raisins
2 garlic cloves, minced	¼ cup chopped pimiento-stuffed olives
½ cup chopped green bell pepper	1 tsp. ground cinnamon
2 lb. ground round	1 tsp. ground cumin
2 (14.5-oz.) cans diced tomatoes with onion and green bell pepper, undrained	1 tsp. salt
	½ tsp. pepper
2 Tbsp. tomato paste	¼ cup slivered almonds, toasted

1. Sauté first 4 ingredients in a large nonstick skillet over medium-high heat until vegetables are tender and beef crumbles and is no longer pink. Drain well.

2. Stir in diced tomatoes and remaining ingredients. Bring to a boil; reduce heat, and simmer, uncovered, 5 minutes.

TO FREEZE IT: Freeze remaining mixture in a labeled zip-top plastic freezer bag up to 1 month.

make it a meal

Serve picadillo inside soft taco shells for a tasty meal. Other typical accompaniments for this Latin dish include white rice and ripe plantains.

PICADILLO-STUFFED PEPPERS

Makes: 4 servings   Hands-on Time: 20 min.   Total Time: 40 min.

4   large green bell peppers
2⅔ cups Picadillo (opposite page)
2   cups cooked rice

½   tsp. ground red pepper
¼   cup (1 oz.) shredded Monterey Jack
     or Manchego cheese

TO THAW IT: Remove Picadillo from the freezer, and thaw in the fridge overnight. Place in a saucepan with ¼ cup water. Gently heat over medium-low heat, stirring occasionally, 15 to 20 minutes or until heated.

1. Preheat oven to 425°.

2. Cut off tops of bell peppers; discard seeds and membranes. Place bell peppers, cut sides up, in an 8-inch baking dish. Microwave, uncovered, at HIGH 6 minutes or just until peppers are tender. Drain peppers, and return to dish.

3. Stir rice and red pepper into heated Picadillo mixture. Spoon stuffing into bell peppers, and sprinkle with cheese.

4. Bake at 425° for 20 minutes or until golden brown.

Manchego cheese, a Spanish cheese made from goat's milk, comes in a wheel shape that's encased in a hard, inedible rind.

test kitchen tip

If you prefer another color pepper, consider using an assortment of colors such as red, yellow, and orange.

SLOPPY JOES

Makes: 8 servings **plus 5 cups for Sloppy Joe Shepherd's Pie**
Hands-on Time: 13 min.   Total Time: 28 min.

3   lb. lean ground beef
2   (14.5-oz.) can diced tomatoes
2½ cups ketchup
1   cup bottled barbecue sauce
2   Tbsp. Worcestershire sauce

4   Tbsp. chopped pickled jalapeños (optional)
2   Tbsp. liquid from pickled jalapeños (optional)
8   hamburger buns, toasted

1. Brown ground beef in a large skillet over medium-high heat, stirring often, 13 minutes or until beef crumbles and is no longer pink; drain well. Return cooked beef to skillet.

2. Stir in tomatoes, next 3 ingredients, and, if desired, jalapeños and liquid. Reduce heat to low, and simmer 15 minutes or until thickened. Divide mixture in half. Serve half of mixture on toasted buns.

TO FREEZE IT: Freeze remaining mixture in a labeled zip-top plastic freezer bag up to 3 months.

Note: We tested with KC Masterpiece Original Barbecue Sauce.

make it a meal

Pair these tasty sandwiches with mixed salad greens topped with a honey mustard vinaigrette. End the meal with store-bought chocolate chip cookies.

SLOPPY JOE SHEPHERD'S PIE

Makes: 8 to 10 servings   Hands-on Time: 10 min.   Total Time: 45 min.

5   cups Sloppy Joes mixture
     (opposite page)
1   (22-oz.) package refrigerated
     mashed potatoes
2   cups (8 oz.) shredded
     Cheddar cheese, divided

⅓   cup sliced green onions
½   tsp. salt
¼   tsp. pepper

TO THAW IT: Remove Sloppy Joes mixture from the freezer, and thaw in the fridge overnight.

1. Preheat oven to 350°. Spoon Sloppy Joes mixture into a lightly greased 13- x 9-inch baking dish.

2. Prepare mashed potatoes according to package directions. Stir in 1 cup shredded Cheddar cheese, sliced green onions, salt, and pepper. Spread over meat mixture in casserole dish, spreading potatoes to edge of dish.

3. Bake at 350° for 25 minutes; sprinkle remaining 1 cup shredded Cheddar cheese on top of potatoes. Bake 5 more minutes or until cheese is melted. Let stand 5 minutes before serving.

This potato-topped shepherd's pie gets extra flavor from the cheese and green onions that are added to the mashed potato crust. Shortcut the crust using refrigerated mashed potatoes.

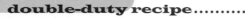

MEATY SPAGHETTI SAUCE

Makes: about 17½ cups, including 4 cups for Stuffed Shells Florentine
Hands-on Time: 58 min.   Total Time: 4 hr., 3 min.

2	lb. lean ground beef	2	cups Burgundy or other dry red wine
2	lb. ground pork or veal	1	cup chopped fresh parsley
1	lb. ground Italian sausage	3	bay leaves
2	large onions, chopped	1½	tsp. salt
2	medium-size green peppers, chopped	2	tsp. dried oregano
5	garlic cloves, minced	2	tsp. dried basil, crushed
2	(28-oz.) cans whole tomatoes, chopped	2	tsp. brown sugar
2	(6-oz.) cans tomato paste		Hot cooked spaghetti
			Grated Parmesan cheese

1. Combine first 6 ingredients in a stockpot. Cook over medium-high heat, stirring constantly, 5 to 8 minutes or until meat crumbles and is no longer pink; drain well. Stir in 2 cups water, tomatoes, and next 8 ingredients. Bring to a boil; cover, reduce heat, and simmer 2 hours, stirring occasionally. Uncover; simmer 1 more hour or to desired consistency, stirring occasionally. Discard bay leaves. Serve over hot spaghetti; sprinkle with Parmesan cheese.

TO FREEZE IT: Freeze remaining sauce in a labeled tightly covered container or zip-top plastic freezer bags up to 3 months.

These rich and cheesy spinach and ricotta-stuffed shells are the ultimate Italian comfort food.

STUFFED SHELLS FLORENTINE

Makes: 8 servings   Hands-on Time: 25 min.   Total Time: 1 hr., 10 min.

24 jumbo macaroni shells
1   (10-oz.) package frozen chopped spinach, thawed and drained
2   cups (8 oz.) shredded mozzarella cheese
2   cups ricotta cheese
½   cup grated Parmesan cheese
3   green onions, minced

2   Tbsp. minced fresh parsley
1   tsp. dried basil
¼   tsp. salt
¼   tsp. ground nutmeg
¼   tsp. pepper
4   cups Meaty Spaghetti Sauce (opposite page)
¼   cup grated Parmesan cheese

TO THAW IT: Remove Meaty Spaghetti Sauce from freezer, and thaw in the fridge overnight. To reheat, cook sauce in a saucepan over medium heat 10 to 12 minutes, until thoroughly heated, stirring occasionally.

1. Preheat oven to 350°. Cook macaroni shells according to package directions; drain well, and set aside. Combine spinach and next 9 ingredients in a large bowl; stir well.

2. Fill each shell with ¼ cup spinach mixture, and place in a lightly greased 13- x 9-inch baking dish. Pour reheated spaghetti sauce over shells; sprinkle with Parmesan cheese. Bake at 350° for 35 to 40 minutes or until hot and bubbly. Let stand 10 minutes before serving.

RAGU ALLA BOLOGNESE

Makes: 4 servings **plus 4 cups sauce for Florentine Lasagna Rolls**
Hands-on Time: 16 min.   **Total Time:** 8 hr., 46 min.

1 lb. lean ground beef	½ cup dry red wine or beef broth
1 lb. ground pork	2 tsp. dried basil
1 (8-oz.) container chopped onion, celery, and green bell pepper	1 tsp. salt
2 medium carrots, finely chopped	¼ tsp. freshly ground black pepper
1 tsp. jarred minced garlic	1 cup milk
2 (14.5-oz.) cans diced tomatoes	8 oz. uncooked fettuccine

1. Cook first 5 ingredients in a large skillet over medium-high heat, stirring constantly, 8 minutes or until meat crumbles and is no longer pink; drain and place in a 3½- to 4-qt. slow cooker.

2. Stir tomatoes and next 4 ingredients into meat mixture. Cover and cook on LOW 8 hours. Stir in milk; cover and cook 30 more minutes.

3. Cook pasta according to package directions; drain. Reserve 4 cups sauce for Florentine Lasagna Rolls, if desired. Serve remaining 4 cups sauce over pasta.

TO FREEZE IT: Cool remaining mixture rapidly. Place in labeled airtight containers, leaving a little headspace at the top of the container. Freeze up to 6 months.

flavor profile

Bolognese is a thick Italian pasta sauce that's made with ground meat, tomatoes, celery, and carrots, and seasoned with garlic and herbs. Some supermarkets have a premixed meatloaf mixture available. Feel free to use that in place of the ground beef and pork—just be sure the meatloaf mixture doesn't contain breadcrumbs.

38

FLORENTINE LASAGNA ROLLS

Makes: 4 to 8 servings   Hands-on Time: 5 min.   Total Time: 48 min.

1   (10-oz.) package frozen chopped
    spinach, thawed and drained
1   (15-oz.) container ricotta cheese
½   cup grated Parmesan cheese
¼   tsp. freshly ground black pepper

8   lasagna noodles, cooked
4   cups warm Ragu alla Bolognese
    (opposite page)
1½ cups (6 oz.) shredded
    mozzarella cheese

This recipe makes 8 lasagna rolls with a meaty sauce. For heartier appetites, plan on 4 servings.

TO THAW IT: Remove Ragu alla Bolognese from freezer, and thaw in fridge overnight. Reheat to a rolling boil on the stovetop for 5 minutes or until heated.

1. Preheat oven to 350°. Stir together first 4 ingredients in a medium bowl. Spread mixture over lasagna noodles; roll up, and place seam sides down in a lightly greased 11- x 7-inch baking dish. Top with sauce. Sprinkle with cheese.
2. Bake, uncovered, at 350° for 35 minutes or until cheese is melted and golden.

Refrigerating the meat in the seasonings before baking adds a delicious flavor to the roast.

OLD-FASHIONED POT ROAST

Makes: 10 to 15 servings plus 5 cups for the Beef-and-Bean Tostadas
Hands-on Time: 35 min.   Total Time: 6 hr., 43 min.

½ cup minced fresh parsley
3 Tbsp. prepared horseradish
3 garlic cloves, minced
1 Tbsp. dried marjoram
1 Tbsp. dried thyme
1 (6- to 7-lb.) chuck roast
4 medium onions, thinly sliced and separated into rings

1 cup Burgundy or other dry red wine
1½ lb. potatoes, peeled and quartered
1 lb. carrots, cut into 2-inch pieces
1 lb. turnips, peeled and cut into chunks
Salt and pepper to taste

1. Preheat oven to 325°. Combine first 5 ingredients; pat over roast. Cover and refrigerate 2 to 4 hours. Combine onion rings and wine in a large Dutch oven; add roast. Bake, covered, at 325° for 2 hours.
2. Add potato, carrot, and turnip; bake, covered, at 325° for 1½ hours. Uncover and bake 20 minutes or until roast is tender. Let stand 15 minutes before serving.
3. Arrange meat and vegetables on a serving platter. Pour pan drippings into a medium saucepan; bring to a boil. Boil 3 minutes. Add salt and pepper. Serve with meat and vegetables.

TO FREEZE IT: Remove remaining meat from bone. Slice or chop meat as desired. Freeze in a labeled airtight container up to 3 months.

BEEF-AND-BEAN TOSTADAS

Makes: 4 servings   Hands-on Time: 22 min.   Total Time: 40 min.

1   medium onion, finely chopped
2   garlic cloves, minced
1   Tbsp. vegetable oil
2   tsp. chili powder
2   tsp. ground cumin
1   tsp. ground coriander
¼   tsp. salt
¼   tsp. ground cinnamon
½   cup tomato juice
1   (16-oz.) can pinto beans, drained, rinsed, and mashed

5   cups sliced Old-Fashioned Pot Roast (opposite page)
8   (6-inch) corn tortillas
1   cup (4 oz.) shredded Cheddar cheese
Freshly ground black pepper to taste
2   cups shredded lettuce
2   green onions, thinly sliced
½   cup salsa
Sour cream (optional)

TO THAW IT: Remove Old-Fashioned Pot Roast from freezer, and thaw in fridge overnight.

1. Preheat oven to 300°. Sauté chopped onion and garlic in oil in a large skillet over medium heat for 6 minutes or until tender. Stir in chili powder and next 5 ingredients. Bring to a boil; reduce heat, and simmer 3 minutes. Stir in mashed beans.

2. Microwave pot roast in a microwave-safe bowl at HIGH 3 to 5 minutes or until thoroughly heated, stirring once.

3. Divide bean mixture among tortillas, spreading to edges. Divide cheese among tortillas; sprinkle with pepper.

4. Place tortillas on ungreased baking sheets. Bake at 300° for 15 minutes or until thoroughly heated. Top with lettuce, green onion, pot roast, and salsa. Serve with sour cream, if desired.

FRENCH ONION POT ROAST

Makes: 8 servings plus 3 cups beef and 1½ cups cooking juices for French Dip Sandwiches
Hands-on Time: 10 min.   Total Time: 8 hr., 10 min.

6	small red potatoes, cut in half	¼	tsp. salt
4	medium carrots, cut into 1-inch pieces	½	tsp. pepper
1	large onion, cut into 6 wedges	1	(10¾-oz.) can French onion soup
1	(4- to 4½-lb.) chuck roast, trimmed and cut in half	1	(10¾-oz.) can golden mushroom soup
		1	bay leaf

1. Place first 3 ingredients in a 5- to 6-qt. slow cooker. Place roast on vegetables, and sprinkle with salt and pepper.

2. Whisk together French onion soup, mushroom soup, and ½ cup water; pour mixture over beef. Add bay leaf. Cover and cook on HIGH 1 hour. Reduce heat to LOW, and cook 7 hours or until tender.

3. Remove roast and vegetables from slow cooker; keep warm. Discard bay leaf. Skim fat from cooking juices. Serve cooking juices with roast and vegetables.

TO FREEZE IT: Remove remaining meat from bone. Slice or chop meat as desired. Freeze in a labeled, airtight container up to 3 months. Freeze 1½ cups cooking juices in a labeled airtight container up to 3 months.

shortcut secret

This recipe comes together quickly with virtually no mess. Begin by lining the slow cooker with a disposable slow cooker liner, and cleanup at the end of the day will be just as effortless.

These sandwiches make a perfect quick-and-easy weeknight meal. Serving them on sturdy bread, such as hoagie rolls, ensures that they will withstand repeated dipping into the sauce.

FRENCH DIP SANDWICHES

Makes: 4 servings   Hands-on Time: 12 min.   Total Time: 12 min.

4 (6-inch) hoagie rolls, cut in half

¼ cup refrigerated horseradish sauce or mayonnaise

3 cups beef from French Onion Pot Roast, shredded (opposite page)

1½ cups cooking juices from French Onion Pot Roast (opposite page)

1 (8-oz.) package provolone cheese slices (8 slices)

TO THAW IT: Remove French Onion Pot Roast and juices from freezer, and thaw in fridge overnight.

1. Preheat broiler.

2. Spread bottom half of each hoagie roll with horseradish sauce, and place on a baking sheet, horseradish sauce side up.

3. Combine shredded roast and cooking juices in a microwave-safe bowl. Cover and cook at HIGH 3 minutes or until thoroughly heated, stirring once. Remove roast with a slotted spoon, and divide on bottom halves of rolls; top each with 2 slices cheese.

4. Broil 5 inches from heat 1 minute or until cheese melts. Cover with top halves of rolls, and serve with reserved juices for dipping.

GRILLED GARLICKY FLANK STEAK

Makes: 4 servings plus half of flank steak for Roast Beef-and-Blue Cheese Panini
Hands-on Time: 30 min.   Total Time: 30 min.

Vegetable cooking spray	½ tsp. kosher salt
¼ cup chopped fresh parsley	½ tsp. freshly ground black pepper
3 Tbsp. minced garlic	1 (2-lb.) flank steak
1 Tbsp. olive oil	Chimichurri

1. Coat cold cooking grate with cooking spray, and place on grill. Preheat grill to 350° to 400° (medium-high) heat.

2. Combine parsley and next 4 ingredients. Rub mixture over flank steak. Marinate in the refrigerator while preparing Chimichurri.

3. Grill steak, covered with grill lid, 8 minutes on each side or until desired degree of doneness. Let stand 10 minutes. Slice steak diagonally across grain into thin slices. Reserve half the slices for Roast Beef-and-Blue Cheese Panini, if desired. Serve steak with Chimichurri.

TO FREEZE IT: Chill remaining sliced flank steak thoroughly. Place in a labeled airtight container, and freeze up to 1 month.

chimichurri

Makes: ½ cup   Hands-on Time: 8 min.   Total Time: 8 min.

¼ cup olive oil vinaigrette	2 Tbsp. chopped fresh cilantro
2 Tbsp. chopped fresh parsley	2 Tbsp. lemon juice

1. Combine all ingredients in a small bowl.

test kitchen tip

Chimichurri is a thick Argentinian sauce and marinade for grilled meats. Some large supermarkets carry the sauce in the condiments aisle, so feel free to substitute a prepared brand for the homemade version if it's available in your local store.

ROAST BEEF-AND-BLUE CHEESE PANINI

Makes: 4 servings   Hands-on Time: 20 min.   Total Time: 25 min.

1   Tbsp. butter
1   large sweet onion, halved and
    thinly sliced
1   (16-oz.) loaf Italian bread
    (such as ciabatta or other crusty
    bread), halved lengthwise

2   Tbsp. olive oil
½   Grilled Garlicky Flank Steak slices
    (opposite page)
1   cup arugula leaves
4   oz. blue cheese, crumbled
2   Tbsp. mayonnaise

TO THAW IT: Remove flank steak from freezer, and thaw in fridge overnight.

1. Preheat the panini grill. Place butter in a large nonstick skillet over medium-high heat until melted. Add onion slices, and cook 10 minutes or until soft and caramelized, stirring often.

2. Brush outsides of bread with olive oil. Place bottom half of bread on panini grill. Top evenly with steak slices, onion slices, and arugula.

3. Combine blue cheese and mayonnaise; spread mixture on cut side of bread top, and place bread over arugula. Cook 5 minutes or until bread is golden. Slice and serve.

test kitchen tip

An indoor electric grill with a lid works just as well as a panini press for this sandwich. If you don't have either, cook your sandwich on the stovetop in a large skillet, pressing down on the sandwich with another large heavy skillet as it cooks. You'll get the same results.

MARGARITA GRILLED PORK TENDERLOIN

Makes: 4 servings plus 1 tenderloin for Loaded Cuban Sandwiches
Hands-on Time: 25 min.   Total Time: 8 hr., 25 min.

1 large garlic clove, minced	½ tsp. chili powder
¼ cup chopped fresh cilantro	2 (1-lb.) pork tenderloins
1 Tbsp. minced jalapeño	Vegetable cooking spray
1½ Tbsp. tequila (optional)	½ tsp. salt
1 tsp. ground cumin	

1. Drop garlic in food chute of food processor while running. Add cilantro, jalapeño, tequila, if desired, cumin, and chili powder. Process until minced. Place in 2 large zip-top plastic freezer bags. Add pork to bags, and seal; marinate 1 in the fridge 8 hours, and label and freeze the other.

2. Coat a cold cooking grate with cooking spray. Preheat grill to 350° to 400° (medium-high) heat. Remove silver skin from tenderloins, leaving a thin layer of fat.

3. Remove pork from marinade, discarding marinade. Sprinkle pork with salt. Grill pork, covered with grill lid, 15 to 18 minutes, turning every 5 minutes, or until a meat thermometer inserted into thickest part of pork registers 155°. Remove from grill; cover with foil, and let stand 5 minutes. Cut tenderloins into thin slices to serve.

TO FREEZE IT: Follow Step 1 to freeze 1 pork tenderloin up to 1 month.

shortcut secret

The marinade in this dish takes only 5 minutes to prepare. Whip up the mixture in the morning, and let the pork marinate in the fridge all day. Then all you'll need to do is grill the meat.

LOADED CUBAN SANDWICHES

Makes: 4 servings   Hands-on Time: 9 min.   Total Time: 13 min.

4 hoagie rolls	¼ lb. thinly sliced deli ham
¼ cup Dijon mustard	8 dill pickle slices
1 Margarita Grilled Pork Tenderloin, thinly sliced (opposite page)	8 slices Swiss cheese

TO THAW IT: Remove pork tenderloin from the freezer, and thaw in the fridge overnight. Prepare for sandwiches by grilling according to Step 2 of Margarita Grilled Pork Tenderloin (opposite page).

1. Preheat broiler. Cut a vertical slit down the center of each hoagie roll, leaving ½ inch of roll attached. Carefully open sides; spread 1 Tbsp. mustard on each roll. Top each roll with pork slices, ham, pickles, and cheese.

2. Place open sandwiches on a baking sheet, and broil 3 to 4 minutes or until cheese is melted and bread is golden.

While this sandwich tastes delicious broiled in the oven, it can also be made in a panini press.

BROWN-SUGARED PORK TENDERLOIN

Makes: 6 servings **plus 1 (2-lb.) package pork tenderloin for Pork Fajitas**
Hands-on Time: 29 min.   Total Time: 9 hr., 9 min.

½   cup cider vinegar
¼   cup firmly packed light brown
     sugar
1   tsp. salt

1   tsp. jarred minced garlic
½   tsp. paprika
½   tsp. dried crushed red pepper
2   (2-lb.) packages pork tenderloin

1. Combine first 6 ingredients, and divide between 2 zip-top plastic freezer bags. Divide pork between bags, and seal; marinate 1 bag in the fridge 8 hours, and freeze the other, if desired.

2. Preheat grill to 350° to 400° (medium-high) heat. Remove tenderloin from bag, reserving marinade. Place marinade in a small saucepan; bring to a boil. Boil 1 minute. Remove from heat, and set aside.

3. Grill tenderloin, uncovered, over medium-high heat 10 to 12 minutes on each side or until a meat thermometer inserted in thickest portion of tenderloin registers 155°, basting often with reserved marinade. Remove from grill; cover with foil, and let stand 10 minutes.

TO FREEZE IT: Follow Step 1 to freeze 1 bag of pork tenderloin up to 1 month.

test kitchen tip

We don't rely on the color of cooked meat to indicate doneness. Always use a meat thermometer inserted into the thickest portion of the tenderloin to be certain meat is cooked to 155°.

PORK FAJITAS

Makes: 6 servings   Hands-on Time: 20 min.   Total Time: 30 min.

2 Brown-Sugared Pork
    Tenderloins (opposite page)
1 red bell pepper, cut into strips
1 green bell pepper, cut into strips
1 medium onion, cut in half
    and vertically sliced

2 Tbsp. fajita seasoning
1 Tbsp. vegetable oil
12 (8-inch) flour tortillas
Toppings: shredded Cheddar cheese,
    guacamole, sour cream, salsa

TO THAW IT: Remove pork tenderloin from the freezer, and thaw in the fridge overnight. Prepare for fajitas by grilling pork tenderloins according to Step 2 of Brown-Sugared Pork Tenderloin (opposite page).

1. Cut pork tenderloins in half lengthwise. Place cut side down, and cut into ¼-inch slices. Combine pork and next 3 ingredients in a large bowl. Sprinkle with fajita seasoning, tossing gently. Let stand 10 minutes.
2. Heat oil in a large skillet over medium-high heat. Add pork mixture; sauté 4 minutes or just until vegetables are crisp-tender.
3. Heat tortillas according to package directions. Serve pork mixture immediately in warm tortillas with toppings.

shortcut secret

Sliced onion can be stored in an airtight container for 2 to 3 days, so save time by slicing a big batch at once for several recipes.

ROAST LOIN OF PORK

Makes: 12 to 14 servings **plus 5 cups for Sesame Noodles with Roast Pork**
Hands-on Time: 15 min.   Total Time: 3 hr., 5 min.

1	(5- to 6-lb.) pork loin roast	2	tsp. ground cumin
4	garlic cloves, minced	½	tsp. pepper
1	Tbsp. dried oregano	½	cup orange juice

1. Preheat oven to 325°. Trim fat from roast. Place roast on a rack in a roasting pan. Combine garlic and next 3 ingredients; rub garlic mixture over roast. Pour orange juice over roast.

2. Insert meat thermometer in roast. Bake, covered, at 325° for 2 hours. Uncover and bake 40 more minutes or until meat thermometer registers 155° (medium). Cover with foil. Let roast stand 10 to 15 minutes before serving.

TO FREEZE IT: Remove remaining meat from bone. Slice or chop meat as desired. Freeze in a labeled airtight container up to 3 months.

SESAME NOODLES WITH ROAST PORK

Makes: 4 servings   Hands-on Time: 15 min.   Total Time: 15 min.

6   oz. vermicelli or thin
    spaghetti, uncooked
¼   cup plus 1 Tbsp. rice wine
    vinegar
2   Tbsp. dark sesame oil,
    divided
1   Tbsp. vegetable oil
2   tsp. hoisin sauce
1   tsp. soy sauce

1   Tbsp. minced fresh ginger
1   garlic clove, minced
5   cups cooked Roast Loin of Pork,
    cut into thin strips
    (opposite page)
½   lb. fresh spinach
3   Tbsp. sesame seeds, toasted
Salt and pepper to taste

TO THAW IT: Remove pork from the freezer, and thaw in the fridge overnight.

1. Cook pasta according to package directions; drain. Place pasta in a large bowl.

2. Combine vinegar, 1 Tbsp. sesame oil, and next 5 ingredients in a small bowl; stir well. Pour half of dressing over pasta, tossing to combine.

3. Heat remaining 1 Tbsp. sesame oil in a large skillet over medium-high heat for 1 minute. Add pork; sauté 3 to 5 minutes or until browned. Add pork to pasta mixture, tossing gently to combine.

4. Remove stems from spinach. Cut spinach into thin strips. Cook in a large nonstick skillet over medium-high heat 3 to 4 minutes or just until spinach wilts. Add spinach to noodle mixture. Sprinkle with sesame seeds, and pour remaining dressing over pasta; toss gently to combine. Add salt and pepper to taste. Serve warm.

BAKED HAM

Makes: 12 servings **plus 2 cups for Ham-and-Bean Soup**
Hands-on Time: 29 min.   Total Time: 3 hr., 49 min.

1   (8-lb.) smoked, ready-to-cook, bone-in ham
1   cup firmly packed light brown sugar
2   Tbsp. cola soft drink
1   Tbsp. yellow mustard
Garnish: fresh sage sprigs

1. Preheat oven to 350°. If necessary, trim skin or excess fat from ham. Stir together brown sugar and next 2 ingredients in a small bowl. Brush half of glaze over ham. Wrap ham tightly with heavy-duty aluminum foil. Place in a foil-lined 13- x 9-inch pan.

2. Bake ham at 350° on lowest oven rack for 2 hours and 40 minutes or until a meat thermometer inserted into ham registers 140°. Uncover and brush with remaining glaze. Bake, uncovered, 20 to 30 more minutes or until lightly browned. Transfer to a serving platter; let stand 20 minutes. Skim fat from pan drippings, and serve with ham. Garnish, if desired.

TO FREEZE IT: Remove remaining meat from bone, reserving bone for Ham-and-Bean Soup (opposite page). Slice or chop the meat as desired. Freeze meat and ham bone in a labeled airtight container up to 3 months.

Serve this family favorite with cornbread muffins for a nourishing weeknight meal.

HAM-AND-BEAN SOUP

Makes: 12 servings   Hands-on Time: 29 min.   Total Time: 1 hr., 25 min.

2   cups ham (opposite page)
2   Tbsp. olive oil
1   large onion, diced
1   bunch green onions, chopped
2   large carrots, diced
2   celery ribs, diced
1   Tbsp. jarred ham-
    flavored soup base
½   tsp. pepper

Reserved ham bone
2   (15-oz.) cans navy beans,
    drained
2   (15-oz.) cans cannellini beans,
    drained
1   (15½-oz.) can black-eyed peas,
    drained
4   large Yukon gold potatoes,
    peeled and diced (about 2 lb.)

TO THAW IT: Remove ham from the freezer, and thaw in the fridge overnight.

1. Cook ham in hot oil in a Dutch oven over medium-high heat, stirring often, 6 to 8 minutes or until browned. Add diced onion and next 5 ingredients, and sauté 5 minutes or until onion is tender.

2. Stir in reserved ham bone, navy beans, and next 3 ingredients; add 4 cups water. Bring to a boil; cover, reduce heat to low, and cook, stirring occasionally, 45 minutes.

Ham-and-Bean Soup with Fresh Spinach:
Prepare recipe as directed, stirring in 1 (5-oz.) package fresh baby spinach just before serving.

EASY BARBECUED CHICKEN

Makes: 12 servings **plus 3 cups for Hearty Brunswick Stew**
Hands-on Time: 29 min.   Total Time: 8 hr., 29 min.

8   (10-oz.) bone-in chicken breasts, skinned
1   medium onion, chopped
1   cup ketchup
¼   cup butter, melted
¼   cup firmly packed light brown sugar
2   Tbsp. cider vinegar
2   Tbsp. Worcestershire sauce
1   Tbsp. yellow mustard
½   tsp. salt
¼   tsp. pepper

1. Place chicken in a 5-qt. slow cooker; top with onion.

2. Whisk together ketchup and remaining ingredients; pour over chicken and onions. Cover and cook on HIGH 1 hour. Reduce heat to LOW, and cook 7 hours. Remove chicken from sauce; cool.

3. Remove chicken from bones, discarding bones. Shred chicken, and stir into sauce.

TO FREEZE IT: Freeze shredded chicken (without sauce) in a labeled airtight container up to 3 months. Freeze the sauce separately in a labeled airtight container up to 3 months.

HEARTY BRUNSWICK STEW

A sure crowd pleaser in the South, this stew is a tasty combination of chicken and vegetables.

Makes: 9 cups   Hands-on Time: 30 min.   Total Time: 30 min.

2   (14-oz.) cans chicken broth
2   cups frozen corn kernels
1   cup frozen baby lima beans
½   (20-oz.) package refrigerated diced potatoes with onions
3   cups Easy Barbecued Chicken and barbecue sauce (opposite page)
1   (8-oz.) can tomato sauce
¼   tsp. salt
¼   tsp. pepper

TO THAW IT: Remove chicken and sauce from the freezer, and thaw in fridge overnight.

1. Combine first 4 ingredients in a Dutch oven over medium-high heat; bring to a boil. Reduce heat, and simmer 15 minutes, stirring occasionally.
2. Stir in Easy Barbecued Chicken with sauce and remaining ingredients; simmer 10 more minutes.

shortcut secret

If you don't have time to make the Easy Barbecued Chicken, use a pound of shredded barbecue chicken from your favorite barbecue restaurant instead.

Cooking the vegetables separate from the chicken ensures that they don't become overcooked.

BRAISED CHICKEN AND VEGETABLES

Makes: 4 servings plus 6 chicken thighs and about 3½ cups vegetable mixture for Creamy Chicken Shepherd's Pie
Hands-on Time: 33 min.   Total Time: 48 min.

14 skinned and boned chicken thighs	2 cups chopped carrots
½ tsp. salt	1 cup chopped celery
¼ tsp. pepper	2 tsp. jarred minced garlic
¼ cup olive oil, divided	1 cup dry white wine or chicken broth
¾ cup all-purpose flour	1 (14-oz.) can chicken broth with roasted garlic
1 (1-lb.) package frozen pearl onions, thawed	¼ cup all-purpose flour
2 (8-oz.) packages sliced fresh mushrooms	

1. Sprinkle chicken thighs with salt and pepper.

2. Heat 2 Tbsp. oil in a large Dutch oven over medium-high heat. While pan is heating, dredge chicken thighs in flour. Cook chicken in 3 batches 2 to 3 minutes on each side or until browned. Remove chicken from pan, and set aside.

3. Heat remaining 2 Tbsp. oil in Dutch oven; add onions and next 4 ingredients. Cook, covered, 5 minutes or until golden, stirring frequently. Add white wine, stirring to loosen particles from bottom of pan; return chicken to pan. Whisk together ½ cup broth and ¼ cup flour, whisking to remove lumps. Add flour mixture and remaining broth to Dutch oven, whisking constantly.

4. Cover, reduce heat to medium, and simmer 15 minutes or until chicken is done and vegetables are tender. Serve 2 thighs per serving for dinner, and reserve 6 chicken thighs and about 3½ cups vegetable mixture for Creamy Chicken Shepherd's Pie.

TO FREEZE IT: Chop reserved chicken thighs into small pieces. Place in a labeled zip-top plastic freezer bag in the freezer. Place 3½ cups vegetable mixture in a labeled zip-top plastic freezer bag. Freeze up to 3 months.

CREAMY CHICKEN SHEPHERD'S PIE

Makes: 4 servings   Hands-on Time: 7 min.   Total Time: 30 min.

6   Braised Chicken thighs,
     chopped (opposite page)
3½ cups braised vegetables
     (opposite page)

1   (24-oz.) package refrigerated
     mashed potatoes

TO THAW IT: Remove chicken and vegetable mixture from the freezer, and thaw in the fridge overnight.

1. Preheat the oven to 375°. Combine chopped chicken and braised vegetable mixture in a medium-size microwave-safe bowl. Place chicken mixture and container of mashed potatoes in the microwave; fold back a small corner of the mashed potatoes to allow steam to escape. Cook at HIGH 3 minutes or until chicken mixture and potatoes are warmed.

2. Pour chicken mixture into a lightly greased 2- to 3-qt. broilerproof baking dish. Top with mashed potatoes. Bake at 375° for 18 minutes or until edges are bubbly. Increase oven temperature to broil. Broil 5 minutes or until potatoes are golden.

Freezing the chicken and vegetables ahead of time makes this 3-ingredient dish super simple. The chicken is a lighter alternative to beef pies.

HERBED DIJON CHICKEN

Makes: 4 servings **plus 4 chicken cutlets for Dijon Chicken Pizza**
Hands-on Time: 27 min.   Total Time: 27 min.

12 (3-oz.) chicken cutlets	½ cup Dijon mustard
½ tsp. salt	1 tsp. dried basil
¼ tsp. pepper	1 tsp. paprika
2 Tbsp. olive oil	½ tsp. dried parsley
½ cup honey	½ tsp. dried oregano

1. Sprinkle chicken cutlets with salt and pepper.

2. Heat olive oil in a large nonstick skillet over medium-high heat. Add chicken; cook in 3 batches 3 minutes on each side or until chicken is cooked through. Remove chicken from pan, and keep warm.

3. Combine honey and remaining 5 ingredients in a small bowl; mix well. Add sauce to pan, and cook over medium heat 2 minutes. Spoon sauce over chicken. Reserve 4 chicken cutlets for Dijon Chicken Pizza, if desired.

TO FREEZE IT: Shred remaining chicken cutlets. Cool completely. Freeze in a labeled airtight container up to 3 months.

make it a meal

For an easy side, prepare frozen mashed sweet potatoes according to package directions. Stir in chopped fresh sage, butter, and salt and pepper to taste.

DIJON CHICKEN PIZZA

Makes: 4 servings   Hands-on Time: 10 min.   Total Time: 20 min.

- ⅔ cup pasta sauce
- 1   (14-oz.) package prebaked Italian cheese-flavored pizza crust
- 4   Herbed Dijon Chicken cutlets, shredded (opposite page)

- 1   cup sliced jarred roasted red bell peppers
- ½   cup chopped pitted kalamata olives
- ½   tsp. dried oregano
- ½   cup (2 oz.) shredded mozzarella cheese

TO THAW IT: Remove chicken from freezer, and thaw in fridge overnight.

1. Preheat oven to 450°. Spread pasta sauce over pizza crust, leaving a 1-inch border. Sprinkle shredded chicken over sauce. Top with peppers, olives, and oregano; sprinkle with cheese.

2. Place pizza directly on oven rack in center of oven. Bake at 450° for 10 minutes or until crust is golden and cheese is melted.

A prepackaged crust, jarred ingredients, and chicken from the freezer help this dish come together faster than delivery pizza.

MARINATED GRILLED CHICKEN THIGHS

Makes: 4 servings **plus 4 thighs for Easy Chicken Chimis**
Hands-on Time: 17 min.   Total Time: 27 min.

2	Tbsp. brown sugar	1	Tbsp. molasses
2	Tbsp. Worcestershire sauce	1	tsp. paprika
3	Tbsp. soy sauce	¾	tsp. garlic salt
1	Tbsp. sesame seeds	¼	tsp. pepper
1	Tbsp. jarred minced garlic	½	cup canola oil
2	Tbsp. sesame oil	12	skinned and boned chicken thighs

1. Combine first 11 ingredients in a large zip-top plastic freezer bag; add chicken. Seal and marinate in the refrigerator 10 minutes. Meanwhile, preheat grill to 350° to 400° (medium-high) heat.

2. Remove chicken from bag, reserving marinade. Place reserved marinade in a saucepan, and bring to a boil; boil 1 minute. Grill chicken, covered with grill lid, 4 to 5 minutes on each side or until done, basting with reserved boiled marinade. Serve immediately.

TO FREEZE IT: Place chicken thighs in labeled zip-top plastic freezer bags, and freeze up to 3 weeks.

Green chiles, stuffed Spanish olives, pickled jalapeño peppers, and a touch of lime add zing to the sauce for this fried burrito.

EASY CHICKEN CHIMIS

Makes: 4 servings   Hands-on Time: 20 min.   Total Time: 20 min.

1 (10¾-oz.) can cream of chicken soup

1 (4.5-oz.) can diced green chiles

2 Tbsp. pimiento-stuffed Spanish olives (about 12)

2 Tbsp. pickled jalapeño peppers

2 Tbsp. lime juice

1 (8-oz.) package cream cheese, softened

1 (8-oz.) package shredded Monterey Jack cheese

1 (1¼-oz.) envelope reduced-sodium taco seasoning mix

4 Marinated Grilled Chicken Thighs, chopped (opposite page)

4 (10-inch) flour tortillas

3 Tbsp. vegetable oil

Toppings: green onions, shredded Cheddar cheese, sour cream

TO THAW IT: Remove chicken from freezer, and thaw in fridge overnight.

1. Process first 5 ingredients in a food processor until smooth, stopping to scrape down sides as needed. Pour soup mixture into a medium saucepan; cook over medium-low heat 5 minutes or until thoroughly heated, stirring occasionally. Remove sauce from heat, and keep warm.

2. Stir together cream cheese and next 3 ingredients. Spoon cream cheese mixture down the center of each tortilla. Fold sides in, and roll up, burrito-style.

3. Heat oil in a large skillet over medium-high heat. Place chimichangas seam-side down in skillet. Fry 2 minutes on each side or until golden.

4. Top with sauce, and serve with desired toppings.

LEMON-THYME ROASTED CHICKEN

Makes: 8 servings **plus 3 cups for Easy Chicken Pot Pie**
Hands-on Time: 15 min.   Total Time: 1 hr., 30 min.

2	Tbsp. dried thyme	1	tsp. salt
6	garlic cloves, pressed	2	(3-lb.) roasting chickens
2	tsp. pepper	2	lemons, halved

1. Preheat oven to 350°. Combine thyme and next 3 ingredients in a small bowl.

2. Remove and discard giblets and necks from chickens. Rinse chickens with cold water; pat dry. Trim excess fat. For each chicken, starting at neck cavity, loosen skin from breast and drumsticks with fingers without totally detaching skin. Rub thyme mixture underneath loosened skin. Carefully replace skin. Place lemon halves inside body cavity. Tie ends of legs together with twine. Tuck wing tips under chicken.

3. Place chickens, breast sides up, on a broiler pan. Insert a meat thermometer into meaty part of a thigh. Bake at 350° for 1 hour or until thermometer registers 165°. Remove chickens from oven; cover with foil, and let stand 15 minutes. Discard skin and lemon.

TO FREEZE IT: Debone the extra chicken. Then chop or shred the meat, and store in a labeled airtight container in the freezer up to 3 months.

EASY CHICKEN POT PIE

Makes: 6 servings   Hands-on Time: 10 min.   Total Time: 45 min.

1   (10¾-oz.) can cream of mushroom soup
1   cup milk, divided
¼   tsp. salt
⅛   tsp. pepper
3   cups chopped Lemon-Thyme Roasted Chicken (opposite page)

1   (16-oz.) package frozen mixed vegetables
Vegetable cooking spray
1   cup all-purpose baking mix
2   Tbsp. egg substitute

TO THAW IT: Remove chicken from freezer, and thaw in the fridge overnight.

1. Preheat oven to 375°. Combine soup, ½ cup milk, salt, and pepper in a medium saucepan over medium-high heat. Bring mixture to a boil; reduce heat, and simmer, uncovered, 1 minute, stirring constantly until smooth.

2. Add chicken and mixed vegetables, stirring well to combine. Return mixture to a boil; cover, reduce heat, and simmer 5 minutes, stirring occasionally. Pour into an 11- x 7-inch baking dish coated with cooking spray.

3. Combine baking mix, remaining ½ cup milk, and egg substitute in a medium bowl; stir until smooth. Spoon batter into 6 equal circular portions over chicken mixture; coat batter with cooking spray. Bake, uncovered, at 375° for 30 minutes; coat with cooking spray a second time, and bake 5 more minutes or until golden.

test kitchen tip

Coating the batter with cooking spray before baking and again near the end of the baking time helps the batter develop a rich golden brown color.

FRENCH ONION SOUP

Makes: 5 cups   Hands-on Time: 5 min.   Total Time: 20 min.

Caramelized Onions (page 24)
2 (10 ½-oz.) cans beef consommé
¼ cup dry white wine
Toppings: Gruyère cheese, croutons

TO THAW IT: Thaw Caramelized Onions in fridge overnight.

1. Place Caramelized Onions, beef consommé, and wine in a 3½- to 4-qt. slow cooker. Cover and cook on HIGH 15 minutes or just until heated. Sprinkle with cheese and croutons.

dinner
express

EGGPLANT PARMESAN LASAGNA

Makes: 8 to 10 servings   Hands-on Time: 1 hr., 10 min.   Total Time: 2 hr., 35 min.

- 2 (26-oz.) jars tomato, garlic, and onion pasta sauce
- ¼ cup chopped fresh basil
- ½ tsp. dried crushed red pepper
- ½ cup whipping cream
- 1 cup grated Parmesan cheese
- 1 large eggplant (about 1½ lb.)
- ½ tsp. salt
- ¼ tsp. black pepper

- 3 large eggs, lightly beaten
- 1 cup all-purpose flour
- 6 Tbsp. olive oil
- 6 lasagna noodles, cooked and drained
- 1 (15-oz.) container low-fat ricotta cheese
- 2 cups (8 oz.) shredded mozzarella cheese

Layers of thin-sliced eggplant replace the meat in this cheesy lasagna recipe. Use the eggplant within a day or two of purchase for the best flavor.

1. Preheat oven to 350°. Cook first 3 ingredients in a 3½-qt. saucepan over medium-low heat 30 minutes. Remove from heat; stir in cream and Parmesan cheese. Set aside.

2. Peel eggplant, and cut crosswise into ¼-inch-thick slices. Sprinkle slices evenly with salt and black pepper. Stir together eggs and 3 Tbsp. water. Dredge eggplant in flour; dip into egg mixture, and dredge again in flour, shaking to remove excess.

3. Cook eggplant, in batches, in 1½ Tbsp. hot oil in a large nonstick skillet over medium-high heat 4 minutes on each side or until golden brown and slightly softened. Drain on paper towels. Repeat with remaining oil and eggplant, wiping skillet clean after each batch, if necessary.

4. Layer 3 lasagna noodles lengthwise in a lightly greased 13- x 9-inch baking dish. Top with one-third tomato sauce mixture and half of eggplant. Dollop half of ricotta cheese on eggplant in dish; top with half of mozzarella. Repeat layers with remaining noodles, one-third sauce mixture, remaining eggplant, and remaining ricotta. Top with remaining one-third sauce mixture and mozzarella cheese.

TO FREEZE IT: Line a 13- x 9-inch baking dish with heavy-duty nonstick aluminum foil, allowing several inches of foil to extend over sides. Prepare recipe as directed in foil-lined dish. Label and freeze unbaked lasagna until firm. Remove from baking dish by holding edges of foil; fold foil over lasagna. Wrap in additional foil, making sure it is tightly sealed. Freeze up to 1 month. To reheat, thaw in fridge overnight. Remove foil, and place lasagna in a lightly greased 13- x 9-inch baking dish. Cover and thaw overnight in the fridge. Bake as directed.

5. Bake at 350° for 35 to 40 minutes or until golden brown. Let stand 20 minutes before serving.

Note: We tested with Classico Organic Tomato, Herbs & Spices Pasta Sauce.

shortcut secret

Six no-cook lasagna noodles may be substituted for the cooked lasagna. Prepare recipe as directed, reserving remaining half of mozzarella for top. Bake, covered, at 350° for 45 minutes. Sprinkle top with reserved cheese; bake, uncovered, for 20 more minutes or until golden brown.

BAKED MACARONI AND CHEESE

Makes: 8 to 10 servings   Hands-on Time: 15 min.   Total Time: 1 hr., 20 min.

Shred your own cheese for this dish since pre-shredded brands don't melt as well in this macaroni and cheese.

1   (8-oz.) package elbow macaroni
16   saltine crackers, finely crushed
1   tsp. seasoned pepper
1   tsp. salt
1   (10-oz.) block extra-sharp Cheddar cheese, shredded

1   (10-oz.) block sharp Cheddar cheese, shredded
6   large eggs, lightly beaten
4   cups milk

1. Preheat oven to 350°. Cook macaroni according to package directions; drain. Layer one-third each of pasta, crackers, pepper, salt, and cheeses in a lightly greased 3-qt. baking dish. Repeat layers twice.

2. Whisk together eggs and milk; pour over pasta mixture.

3. Bake at 350° for 55 to 60 minutes or until golden and set. Let stand 10 minutes before serving.

TO FREEZE IT: Prepare and bake dish as directed. Cool quickly by chilling baking dish in a bath of ice water in the sink for 10 to 15 minutes. Package in labeled individual dishes, or freeze in baking dish for up to 4 months. To reheat, place frozen casserole in a 400° oven for 1 hour to 1½ hours or until temperature reaches 165°.

MEATLESS CHILI

Makes: 4 servings   Hands-on Time: 5 min.   Total Time: 18 min.

Vegetable cooking spray
1   large onion, chopped
2   tsp. jarred minced garlic
1   (16-oz.) can chili-hot beans, undrained
1   (14.5-oz.) can no-salt-added diced tomatoes, undrained

1   tsp. chili powder
1   tsp. ground cumin
12 oz. frozen vegetable and grain protein crumbles (about 3 cups)
Toppings: oyster crackers, sour cream, shredded cheese, sliced green onions

1. Coat a 4-qt. saucepan with cooking spray. Place pan over medium-high heat. Add onion and garlic; sauté 3 minutes. Add beans and next 3 ingredients. Bring to a boil, stirring occasionally; reduce heat, and simmer 5 minutes. Add protein crumbles, and cook 3 minutes or until thoroughly heated. Serve with desired toppings.

TO FREEZE IT: Cool quickly to room temperature. Place in a labeled airtight container, leaving at least 1 inch headspace, and freeze up to 6 months. To reheat, remove chili from freezer, and bring to a full boil until heated.

make it a meal

Try this chili as a burrito filling. Just spoon it onto a warm flour tortilla, sprinkle with shredded lettuce and cheese, and roll up the tortilla.

QUESO POTATO CHOWDER

Makes: 6 servings   Hands-on Time: 40 min.   Total Time: 1 hr., 10 min.

A Mexican spin on a classic cheese-potato soup, this crowd-pleasing dish gets its zip from poblano peppers.

¼ cup butter
1 cup red bell pepper, finely chopped
1 cup onion, finely chopped
3 poblano peppers, seeded and finely chopped
2 garlic cloves, minced
½ (20-oz.) package refrigerated Southwestern-style hash brown potatoes
¼ tsp. ground cumin
2 (14-oz.) cans low-sodium fat-free chicken broth
⅓ cup all-purpose flour
1½ cups milk
1 cup half-and-half
1 cup (4 oz.) shredded asadero cheese*
1 cup (4 oz.) shredded sharp Cheddar cheese
Toppings: corn tortilla chips, finely chopped red bell pepper, finely chopped red onion, sliced jalapeño peppers, chopped fresh cilantro

1. Melt butter in a Dutch oven over medium-high heat; add bell pepper and next 3 ingredients, and sauté 4 to 5 minutes or until tender. Add potatoes and cumin, and sauté 5 minutes or until browned and tender. Gradually stir in broth, stirring to loosen particles from bottom of Dutch oven. Bring to a boil; cover, reduce heat to low, and simmer 25 minutes.

2. Whisk together flour and next 2 ingredients. Stir into potato mixture, and cook over medium heat, stirring constantly, 5 minutes or until thickened. Reduce heat to low.

3. Add cheeses, and cook, stirring constantly, until cheeses melt and mixture is thoroughly heated. Serve with desired toppings.

*Monterey Jack cheese may be substituted.

Note: We tested with Simply Potatoes Southwest Style Hash Browns.

TO FREEZE IT: Place the pot of soup in a bath of ice water in the sink to cool. Stir the soup often to help release the heat. Ladle into gallon- or quart-size zip-top plastic freezer bags. Remove any excess air, and seal; label and freeze up to 1 month. To reheat, thaw soup overnight in fridge, and simmer over low heat, stirring occasionally.

Queso-Broccoli Potato Chowder: Prepare recipe as directed. Place 1 (12-oz.) package fresh broccoli florets in a 1-qt. microwave-safe glass bowl. Cover tightly with plastic wrap; fold back a small edge to allow steam to escape. Microwave at HIGH 3 to 4½ minutes or until broccoli is crisp-tender, stirring after 2 minutes. Drain and pat dry. Stir hot broccoli into chowder. Top each serving with sautéed chopped ham. Makes: 12 cups; Hands-on Time: 40 min.; Total Time: 1 hr., 15 min.

CHUNKY VEGETABLE SOUP

Makes: 35 cups   Hands-on Time: 20 min.   Total Time: 40 min.

2 lb. ground chuck
1 small sweet onion, chopped
1 tsp. salt
½ tsp. pepper
3 (14-oz.) cans low-sodium beef broth
3 (29-oz.) cans mixed vegetables with potatoes, drained and rinsed
3 (14½-oz.) cans diced new potatoes, drained and rinsed

1 (15-oz.) can sweet peas with mushrooms and pearl onions, drained and rinsed
2 (24-oz.) jars tomato, herbs, and spices pasta sauce
1 (14½-oz.) can diced tomatoes with sweet onion
Garnish: chopped fresh parsley

1. Brown ground chuck and onion, in batches, in a large Dutch oven over medium-high heat, stirring constantly, 5 to 8 minutes or until meat crumbles and is no longer pink. Drain well, and return to Dutch oven. Stir in salt, pepper, and beef broth; bring to a boil.

2. Stir in mixed vegetables and remaining ingredients except garnish. Bring to a boil; cover, reduce heat, and simmer at least 20 minutes or until thoroughly heated. Garnish, if desired.

Note: We tested with Classico Organic Tomato, Herbs & Spices Pasta Sauce.

TO FREEZE IT: Freeze in meal-size portions in zip-top plastic freezer bags. Fold top edge down, and place in a large glass measuring cup to stabilize the bag while filling. Seal the bag, removing as much air as possible; label and freeze up to 3 months. Thaw soup in the fridge. Reheat over medium-low heat.

make it a meal
Pack this soup in thermoses for kids to take for school lunches—it's a great way to add more vegetables into their meals. Freezing the soup in individual portions makes it easy.

TEX-MEX LASAGNA

Makes: 8 servings   Hands-on Time: 20 min.   Total Time: 35 min.

1½ lb. ground round
1 tsp. jarred minced garlic
1 (15-oz.) can black beans, drained and rinsed
1 (8-oz.) package shredded sharp Cheddar cheese, divided
2 Tbsp. chili powder
½ tsp. ground cumin
1 (10-oz.) can diced tomatoes with green chiles, drained
1 (8-oz.) container sour cream
1 (16-oz.) bottle chunky salsa
6 (10-inch) flour tortillas

1. Preheat oven to 425°. Brown beef and garlic in a large nonstick skillet over medium-high heat, stirring constantly, 5 to 8 minutes or until beef crumbles and is no longer pink; drain.

2. Combine beef mixture, black beans, 1 cup cheese, and next 5 ingredients. Line a lightly greased 13- x 9-inch baking dish with 2 tortillas. Spoon one-third of beef mixture over tortillas. Repeat layers twice. Sprinkle with remaining cheese.

3. Bake at 425° for 15 minutes or until cheese melts.

TO FREEZE IT: Bake as directed, and cool quickly to room temperature. Spoon into labeled individual dishes, or freeze in casserole dish up to 6 months. To reheat, thaw in the fridge overnight. Bake at 375° for 1 hour or until casserole reaches 165°.

test kitchen tip

Both salsa and diced tomatoes with green chiles come in varying heat levels to suit your taste.

shortcut secret

If you'd rather use fresh garlic than jarred, use a garlic press. Place a peeled clove in the gadget, and press to force it through the tiny holes.

HOME-STYLE GROUND BEEF CASSEROLE

Makes: 6 servings   Hands-on Time: 23 min.   Total Time: 1 hr., 18 min.

1   lb. ground round
1   (14½-oz.) can diced tomatoes with basil, garlic, and oregano, undrained
1   (10-oz.) can diced tomatoes and green chiles, undrained
1   (6-oz.) can tomato paste
1   tsp. salt
½   tsp. dried Italian seasoning
¼   tsp. pepper
3   cups uncooked medium egg noodles

5   green onions, chopped
1   (8-oz.) container sour cream
1   (3-oz.) package cream cheese, softened
1   cup (4 oz.) shredded sharp Cheddar cheese
1   cup (4 oz.) shredded Parmesan cheese
1   cup (4 oz.) shredded mozzarella cheese

This family-favorite ground beef casserole features egg noodles combined with a variety of canned tomatoes and four types of cheeses, providing a delicious comfort food supper for busy weeknights.

1. Brown ground round in a large skillet over medium heat, stirring constantly, 5 to 8 minutes or until meat crumbles and is no longer pink; drain. Stir in both cans diced tomatoes and next 4 ingredients. Bring to a boil; reduce heat, and simmer, uncovered, 5 minutes. Remove from heat; set aside.

2. Preheat oven to 350°. Prepare egg noodles according to package directions. Stir together hot cooked noodles, chopped green onions, sour cream, and cream cheese until blended.

3. Spoon egg noodles into a lightly greased 13- x 9-inch baking dish. Top with beef mixture; sprinkle with cheeses in order listed.

TO FREEZE IT: Label and freeze assembled, unbaked casserole up to 1 month. Thaw in fridge overnight. Let stand 30 minutes; bake as directed.

4. Bake, covered, at 350° for 35 minutes. Uncover and bake 5 more minutes. Let stand 10 to 15 minutes before serving.

BEEFY MINESTRONE SOUP

Makes: 6 servings   Hands-on Time: 3 min.   Total Time: 13 min.

⅔ cup uncooked ditalini (very short, tube-shaped macaroni)

2 (14½-oz.) cans low-sodium fat-free beef broth

1 (14½-oz.) can no-salt-added stewed tomatoes, undrained

1 large zucchini

1 (15½-oz.) can cannellini beans or other white beans, drained and rinsed

2 tsp. dried Italian seasoning

8 oz. rare deli roast beef, sliced ¼ inch thick and diced

1. Combine first 3 ingredients in a large saucepan; cover and bring to a boil over high heat.

2. Cut zucchini in half lengthwise, and slice. Add zucchini, beans, and Italian seasoning to pasta; cover, reduce heat, and simmer 6 minutes. Add beef, and cook 4 minutes or until pasta is tender.

TO FREEZE IT: Cool soup to room temperature (approximately 30 minutes). Transfer to a labeled airtight container, leaving at least 1 inch headspace. Freeze up to 1 month. To reheat, thaw soup overnight in fridge, and simmer over low heat, stirring occasionally.

flavor profile

Zucchini is abundant and inexpensive during its peak months of June through late August. Select firm, unblemished zucchini. Smaller ones are tender and have bright flavor, while large ones tend to be watery and seedy (those are best used in baked goods that benefit from their moisture). You can store zucchini in a perforated plastic bag in the refrigerator crisper drawer for up to 3 days.

NOODLE-AND-SPINACH CASSEROLE

Makes: 8 to 10 servings   Hands-on Time: 15 min.   Total Time: 45 min.

- 1 (8-oz.) package wide egg noodles
- 1½ lb. ground beef
- 2 garlic cloves, minced
- ½ tsp. salt
- ½ tsp. pepper
- 1 (26-oz.) jar spaghetti sauce
- 1 tsp. dried Italian seasoning
- 1 (10-oz.) package frozen chopped spinach, thawed and drained
- 2 cups (8 oz.) shredded Monterey Jack cheese
- 1½ cups sour cream
- 1 large egg, lightly beaten
- 1 tsp. garlic salt
- 1½ cups (6 oz.) shredded Parmesan cheese

1. Preheat oven to 350°. Cook noodles according to package directions; set aside.

2. Brown beef and next 3 ingredients in a large nonstick skillet over medium heat, stirring constantly, 5 to 8 minutes or until beef crumbles and is no longer pink. Drain and return to skillet. Stir in spaghetti sauce and Italian seasoning.

3. Combine spinach and next 4 ingredients. Fold in noodles; spoon mixture into a lightly greased 13- x 9-inch baking dish. Sprinkle with half of Parmesan cheese. Top with beef mixture and remaining Parmesan cheese.

4. Bake at 350° for 30 minutes or until bubbly and golden.

TO FREEZE IT: Bake as directed. Let cool; cover, label, and freeze up to 1 month. Let thaw overnight in fridge. Bake, covered, at 350° for 30 minutes. Uncover and bake 10 more minutes.

MAKE-AHEAD BEEFY LASAGNA

A container of refrigerated pesto adds distinctive flavor to this classic beef-and-cheese lasagna.

Makes: 8 servings   Hands-on Time: 20 min.   Total Time: 1 hr., 30 min.

12 uncooked lasagna noodles
1 (24-oz.) container 4% small-curd cottage cheese
1 (15-oz.) container ricotta cheese
2 large eggs, lightly beaten
½ cup refrigerated pesto
1 tsp. salt

2½ cups (10 oz.) shredded mozzarella cheese, divided
1 lb. lean ground beef
½ cup finely chopped onion
2 (24-oz.) jars tomato-and-basil pasta sauce

1. Preheat oven to 375°. Prepare noodles according to package directions.

2. Meanwhile, stir together cottage cheese and next 4 ingredients. Stir in 1 cup mozzarella cheese.

3. Brown ground beef and onion in a large skillet over medium-high heat, stirring often, 6 to 7 minutes or until meat crumbles and is no longer pink; drain. Stir in pasta sauce.

4. Layer 1 cup beef mixture, 3 noodles, and 2½ cups cottage cheese mixture in a lightly greased 13- x 9-inch baking dish. Top with 3 noodles, 2 cups beef mixture, and 3 more noodles. Top with remaining cottage cheese mixture, 3 noodles, and beef mixture. Sprinkle with remaining 1½ cups mozzarella cheese.

TO FREEZE IT: Label and freeze assembled, unbaked lasagna up to 3 months. To prepare, thaw in the fridge overnight. Let stand 30 minutes; bake as directed.

5. Bake, covered, at 375° for 40 to 45 minutes. Uncover and bake 20 minutes or until cheese is browned. Let stand 10 to 15 minutes before serving.

Note: We tested with Classico Di Napoli Tomato & Basil Pasta Sauce and LeGrand Garden Pesto and Buitoni Reduced Fat Pesto with Basil.

TOMATO-BASIL MEATLOAF

Makes: 6 to 8 servings   Hands-on Time: 10 min.   Total Time: 1 hr., 20 min.

1 lb. ground chuck
1 lb. lean ground pork
1 (14.5-oz.) can diced tomatoes with basil, oregano, and garlic, drained
⅓ cup marinara sauce
⅓ cup Italian-seasoned breadcrumbs

1 large egg, lightly beaten
1 tsp. salt
1 tsp. pepper
½ cup (2 oz.) shredded mozzarella cheese
Garnishes: 2 plum tomatoes, chopped; small fresh basil leaves

1. Preheat oven to 375°. Stir together ground chuck and pork in a large bowl.

2. Process diced tomatoes in a blender or food processor 5 seconds or until slightly chunky, stopping to scrape down sides as needed. Stir tomatoes, marinara sauce, and next 4 ingredients into ground beef mixture just until combined. Shape into a 9- x 5-inch loaf.

TO FREEZE IT: Cover meatloaf with plastic wrap and aluminum foil, label, and freeze up to 2 months. To prepare, remove from freezer, and thaw in fridge 24 hours. Uncover and proceed with recipe as directed.

3. Place meatloaf on a wire rack in a foil-lined jelly-roll pan.

4. Bake at 375° for 1 hour. Top with mozzarella cheese, and bake 15 more minutes or until center is no longer pink. Let stand 5 minutes before serving. Garnish, if desired.

make it a meal

If you're looking for a new way to serve meatloaf, try it as a sandwich. Top bread slices with slices of meatloaf, mayonnaise, tomato, lettuce, or whatever sandwich toppings you like. This is a great use for leftover meatloaf.

HAMBURGER STEAK WITH SWEET ONION-MUSHROOM GRAVY

Makes: 4 servings   Hands-on Time: 15 min.   Total Time: 23 min.

¼ cup fine, dry breadcrumbs	1 (1.2-oz.) envelope brown gravy mix
1 lb. ground round	1 Tbsp. vegetable oil
1 large egg, lightly beaten	1 (8-oz.) package sliced fresh
2 garlic cloves, minced	mushrooms
½ tsp. salt	1 medium-size sweet onion,
½ tsp. freshly ground black pepper	halved and thinly sliced

Convenience products like packaged dry breadcumbs, gravy mix, and sliced fresh mushrooms help this recipe come together in just 15 minutes.

1. Place breadcrumbs in a mixing bowl; add ground round and next 4 ingredients. Combine until blended, using your hands. Shape into 4 (4-inch) patties.

TO FREEZE IT: Wrap each patty individually in plastic wrap, place in a large zip-top plastic freezer bag, label, and freeze up to 3 months. To thaw, remove from freezer, thaw frozen patties in the fridge overnight, and proceed with Steps 2 and 3.

2. Whisk together gravy mix and 1½ cups water.

3. Cook patties in hot oil in a large skillet over medium-high heat 2 minutes on each side or just until browned. Remove patties from skillet. Add mushrooms and onion to skillet, and sauté 6 minutes or until tender. Stir in prepared gravy, and bring to a light boil. Return patties to skillet, and spoon gravy over each patty. Cover, reduce heat to low, and simmer 8 to 10 minutes.

Bottled Italian dressing provides a simple, flavorful marinade for these grilled flank steak-filled fajitas. Use store-bought pico de gallo or make your own ahead of time.

BEEF FAJITAS WITH PICO DE GALLO

Makes: 6 servings   Hands-on Time: 10 min.   Total Time: 8 hr., 28 min.

1 (8-oz.) bottle zesty Italian dressing
3 Tbsp. fajita seasoning
2 (1-lb.) flank steaks
12 (6-inch) flour tortillas, warmed

Shredded Monterey Jack cheese
Pico de gallo
Garnishes: lime slices, fresh cilantro, guacamole, tortilla chips

1. Combine Italian dressing and fajita seasoning in a shallow dish or zip-top plastic freezer bag; add steaks. Cover or seal, and chill 8 hours, turning occasionally. Remove steak from marinade, discarding marinade.

TO FREEZE IT: Freeze marinated steak in a labeled zip-top plastic freezer bag or an airtight container up to 1 month. To prepare, thaw in fridge overnight, and proceed with recipe as directed.

2. Preheat grill to 350° to 400° (medium-high) heat. Grill steaks, covered with grill lid, 8 minutes. Turn and grill 5 more minutes or to desired degree of doneness. Remove steaks, and cover with aluminum foil. Let stand 10 minutes.
3. Cut steaks diagonally across the grain into very thin slices, and serve with tortillas, cheese, and pico de gallo. Garnish, if desired.

Note: We tested with McCormick Fajita Seasoning.

CUMIN-CRUSTED PORK CUTLETS

Makes: 4 to 6 servings   Hands-on Time: 10 min.   Total Time: 22 min.

3   (2.8-oz.) whole wheat bread slices
2   Tbsp. self-rising yellow cornmeal mix
½   tsp. ground cumin
8   thinly sliced boneless pork loin chops (about 1¼ lb.)

½   tsp. salt
¼   tsp. pepper
1   large egg
2   Tbsp. whole grain mustard
¼   cup olive oil

1. Preheat oven to 200°. Process bread in a food processor until finely crumbled. Combine breadcrumbs, cornmeal mix, and cumin in a shallow bowl.

2. Sprinkle pork chops with salt and pepper. Whisk together egg, mustard, and 2 Tbsp. water until blended. Dip pork in egg mixture; dredge in breadcrumb mixture, pressing to adhere.

TO FREEZE IT: Lay 4 pork chops on the bottom of a labeled gallon-size zip-top plastic freezer bag, top with a piece of wax paper, and then lay remaining 4 pork chops in the bag. Freeze up to 3 months. To proceed, place frozen cutlets in the nonstick skillet as directed.

3. Cook half of pork in 2 Tbsp. hot oil in a large nonstick skillet over medium heat 3 to 4 minutes on each side or until golden brown. Keep warm in a 200° oven. Repeat procedure with remaining pork and oil. Serve warm.

make it a meal

Serve with cole slaw (see Freezer Slaw, page 188) and refrigerated mashed potatoes.

BACON-WRAPPED PORK TENDERLOIN

Makes: 4 servings   Hands-on Time: 10 min.   Total Time: 50 min.

1   (1-lb.) pork tenderloin
1   tsp. steak seasoning

3   bacon slices, cut in half
     crosswise

1. Preheat oven to 425°. Remove silver skin from pork, leaving a thin layer of fat. Sprinkle seasoning over pork. Wrap pork with bacon slices, and secure with wooden picks. Place pork on a lightly greased wire rack in an aluminum foil-lined roasting pan.

TO FREEZE IT: Wrap tenderloin in aluminum foil, place in a labeled zip-top plastic freezer bag, and freeze up to 3 months. To proceed, thaw tenderloin in the fridge for 24 hours, and prepare recipe as directed.

2. Bake at 425° for 25 minutes or until a meat thermometer inserted into thickest portion registers 155°. Increase oven temperature to broil. Broil 5 inches from heat 3 to 5 minutes or until bacon is crisp. Remove from oven; cover pork with foil, and let stand 10 minutes.

Note: We tested with McCormick Grill Mates Montreal Steak Seasoning.

Everything's better with bacon, and this recipe is no exception! Go ahead and season the other tenderloin in the package with your favorite spice blend. Wrap and freeze to jump-start a second meal.

SPAGHETTI WITH SAUSAGE AND PEPPERS

This easy-to-prepare family favorite stays fresh in your freezer for up to two months.

Makes: 4 servings   Hands-on Time: 20 min.   Total Time: 20 min.

8   oz. uncooked spaghetti
1   (1-lb.) package mild Italian sausage, casings removed
1   medium onion, chopped
1   medium-size green bell pepper, chopped
1   medium-size red or yellow bell pepper, chopped
2   to 3 garlic cloves, minced
1   Tbsp. olive oil
1   (28-oz.) can diced tomatoes with basil, garlic, and oregano
¼   tsp. salt
¼   tsp. pepper
½   cup grated Parmesan cheese
Garnish: shaved Parmesan cheese

1. Prepare pasta according to package directions.

2. Meanwhile, brown sausage in a large Dutch oven over medium-high heat, stirring constantly, 8 to 10 minutes or until meat crumbles and is no longer pink. Remove sausage and drippings from Dutch oven, and drain well on paper towels.

3. Sauté onion and next 3 ingredients in hot oil in Dutch oven over medium-high heat 5 to 6 minutes or until vegetables are crisp-tender. Stir in tomatoes, salt, and pepper; cook 4 minutes or until thoroughly heated. Stir in sausage, pasta, and grated cheese. Transfer mixture to a serving platter, and garnish, if desired. Serve immediately.

TO FREEZE IT: Prepare recipe as directed. Cool 30 minutes. Place pasta mixture in a 13- x 9-inch baking dish. Cover tightly with plastic wrap and aluminum foil. Label and freeze up to 2 months. To reheat, thaw in fridge 24 hours. Preheat oven to 350°. Remove and discard plastic wrap and aluminum foil. Cover with aluminum foil, and bake at 350° for 40 to 45 minutes or until thoroughly heated.

Spaghetti with Turkey Sausage and Peppers: Substitute 1 (1-lb.) package Italian turkey sausage for mild Italian sausage. Remove and discard casings from sausage. Increase olive oil to 2 Tbsp. Cook sausage in 1 Tbsp. hot oil as directed in Step 2. Discard any drippings in Dutch oven. Proceed with recipe as directed, sautéing onion and next 3 ingredients in remaining 1 Tbsp. oil.

CHEESY SAUSAGE-AND-TOMATO MANICOTTI

Makes: 6 servings   Hands-on Time: 20 min.   Total Time: 1 hr., 5 min.

- 1 (8-oz.) package uncooked manicotti noodles
- 1 (15-oz.) can tomato sauce
- 1 (14.5-oz.) can diced tomatoes with garlic, oregano, and basil
- 1 lb. Italian sausage, casings removed
- 1 (8-oz.) package cream cheese
- 1 cup ricotta cheese
- 4 cups (16 oz.) shredded mozzarella cheese, divided
- ½ cup chopped fresh parsley (optional)

1. Preheat oven to 350°. Cook pasta according to package directions. Process tomato sauce and diced tomatoes in a blender 20 seconds or until smooth. Set aside.

2. Brown sausage in a large skillet over medium-high heat, stirring constantly, 8 to 10 minutes or until meat crumbles and is no longer pink; drain. Stir in cream cheese, ricotta cheese, and 2 cups mozzarella cheese. Spoon into manicotti shells; arrange stuffed shells in lightly greased 13- x 9-inch baking dish.

3. Pour tomato mixture over shells; sprinkle with remaining 2 cups mozzarella cheese.

TO FREEZE IT: Label and freeze assembled, unbaked casserole up to 1 month. Thaw in the fridge overnight; bake, covered, at 350° for 30 minutes. Uncover and bake 15 more minutes or until cheese is melted and bubbly. If you prefer a smaller casserole, use 2 (11- x 7-inch) baking dishes. Proceed as directed.

4. Bake at 350° for 20 minutes or until cheese is melted and bubbly. Let casserole stand 10 minutes before serving. Sprinkle top with chopped fresh parsley, if desired.

Ground Beef-and-Tomato Manicotti: Substitute 1 lb. lean ground beef for sausage. Stir in ½ tsp. dried Italian seasoning, 1 tsp. salt, 1 tsp. pepper, and 1 tsp. fennel seed. Proceed as directed.

shortcut secret

For a faster way to fill the manicotti shells, simply slice each noodle lengthwise, fill, and fold the noodle back together. Then place the cut side down in the dish.

SOUTHWEST SAUSAGE CHILI

Makes: 12½ cups   Hands-on Time: 10 min.   Total Time: 26 min.

2 lb. ground Italian sausage
½ cup minced onion
2 (16-oz.) cans kidney beans, drained and rinsed
2 (7-oz.) cans whole kernel corn with sweet red pepper
2 (15-oz.) cans tomato sauce

1⅓ cups salsa
2 tsp. chili powder
½ tsp. freshly ground black pepper
½ tsp. ground cumin
¼ tsp. salt
Toppings: shredded cheese, sour cream (optional)

1. Brown sausage and onion in a Dutch oven over medium-high heat, stirring constantly, 8 to 10 minutes or until sausage crumbles and is no longer pink; drain.

2. Stir in beans, 1⅓ cups water, and next 7 ingredients. Bring to a boil over medium-high heat. Reduce heat to medium; simmer, uncovered, for 12 minutes or until thoroughly heated, stirring often.

3. Serve chili with shredded cheese and sour cream, if desired.

TO FREEZE IT: Freeze soup in meal-size portions in zip-top plastic freezer bags. Fold top edge down, and place in a large glass measuring cup to stabilize the bag while filling. Seal the bag, removing as much air as possible; label and freeze up to 3 months. Thaw soup in the fridge. Reheat over medium-low heat.

SAUSAGE-AND-CHEESE CALZONE

Makes: 8 to 10 servings   Hands-on Time: 15 min.   Total Time: 45 min.

- 1 lb. mild or hot Italian sausage, casings removed
- 1 medium onion, halved and sliced
- 1 large yellow or red bell pepper, sliced
- 1 (15-oz.) container low-fat ricotta cheese
- 2 large eggs
- 1½ tsp. salt-free herb-and-spice seasoning
- 2 (13.8-oz.) cans refrigerated pizza crust dough
- ½ cup pizza sauce
- 1 (8-oz.) package shredded Italian six-cheese blend, divided

1. Preheat oven to 425°. Sauté first 3 ingredients in a large nonstick skillet over medium-high heat 10 minutes or until meat crumbles and is no longer pink and vegetables are lightly browned. Remove from skillet, and drain well.

2. Stir together ricotta cheese, eggs, and seasoning.

3. Unroll 1 can of dough on a lightly greased baking sheet. Stretch dough into a 13- x 10-inch rectangle. Spoon ¼ cup pizza sauce, 1 cup ricotta mixture, and half of sausage mixture on half of rectangle, leaving a 1-inch border. Sprinkle with 1 cup cheese. Moisten edges with water; fold dough over, pressing and crimping edges to seal. Cut 3 (1-inch) slits on top of dough to allow steam to escape. Repeat procedure with remaining dough, pizza sauce, ricotta mixture, sausage mixture, and cheese.

4. Bake at 425° for 24 to 26 minutes or until golden. Serve with additional warm pizza sauce, if desired.

TO FREEZE IT: Wrap leftover calzones individually in plastic wrap, and place in labeled zip-top plastic freezer bags. Store in single layers. To reheat, thaw in refrigerator overnight. Preheat oven to 350°. Remove plastic wrap, and place calzones on baking sheet 2 inches apart. Bake at 350° for 20 minutes or until thoroughly heated.

Cheesy Mexican Calzones: Prepare recipe as directed, substituting 1 lb. ground beef and ½ tsp. salt for sausage, 2 tsp. salt-free Southwest chipotle seasoning, and ¾ tsp. salt for salt-free herb-and-spice seasoning, and shredded Mexican four-cheese blend for shredded Italian six-cheese blend.

Note: We tested with Mrs. Dash Southwest Chipotle Seasoning Blend.

JAMBALAYA

Makes: 6 servings   Hands-on Time: 15 min.   Total Time: 35 min.

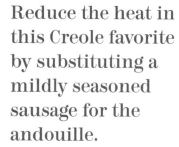

Reduce the heat in this Creole favorite by substituting a mildly seasoned sausage for the andouille.

1   lb. andouille sausage, cut into ¼-inch-thick slices
1   (10-oz.) package frozen vegetable seasoning blend
1   (32-oz.) container low-sodium chicken broth
1   (14.5-oz.) can fire-roasted diced tomatoes with garlic
2   cups uncooked long-grain rice
2   Tbsp. chopped fresh parsley
1   tsp. Cajun seasoning
2   tsp. Worcestershire sauce
⅛   tsp. ground red pepper (optional)
2   Tbsp. thinly sliced green onions

1. Cook sausage in a large Dutch oven over medium-high heat, stirring frequently, 8 to 10 minutes or until browned. Remove sausage with a slotted spoon; drain sausage on paper towels. Reserve drippings in pan.

2. Add vegetable seasoning blend to hot drippings in Dutch oven, and sauté 3 to 5 minutes or until thoroughly heated. Add broth, next 5 ingredients, sausage, and, if desired, ground red pepper. Bring to a boil; cover, reduce heat to low, and cook 18 to 20 minutes or until rice is tender and liquid is absorbed. Top with green onions, and serve immediately.

Note: We tested with McKenzie's Seasoning Blend frozen vegetables and Hunt's Fire Roasted Diced Tomatoes With Garlic.

TO FREEZE IT: Prepare recipe as directed, omitting green onions. Cool rapidly. Place jambalaya in a labeled airtight container, leaving 1-inch headspace, and freeze 4 to 6 months. To reheat, thaw in fridge overnight. Reheat on stovetop until temperature reaches 165°. Top with green onions.

Spicy bits of hickory-smoked sausage kick up the heat in this classic Southern dish.

OKRA-AND-CORN MAQUE CHOUX

Makes: 8 servings   Hands-on Time: 18 min.   Total Time: 18 min.

- ¼ lb. spicy smoked sausage, diced
- ½ cup chopped sweet onion
- ½ cup chopped green bell pepper
- 2 garlic cloves, minced
- 3 cups fresh corn kernels
- 1 cup sliced fresh okra
- 1 cup peeled, seeded, and diced tomato (about ½ lb.)
- Salt and freshly ground pepper to taste

1. Sauté sausage in a large skillet over medium-high heat 3 minutes or until browned. Add onion, bell pepper, and garlic, and sauté 5 minutes or until tender. Add corn, okra, and tomato; cook, stirring often, 10 minutes. Season with salt and pepper to taste.

Note: We tested with Conecuh Original Hot and Spicy Smoked Sausage.

TO FREEZE IT: Let maque choux cool completely, and freeze in a labeled zip-top plastic freezer bag up to 1 month. To reheat, thaw overnight in fridge. Heat in a medium saucepan over medium heat, stirring often, until warm.

SPICY HAM-AND-GREENS QUICHE

Makes: 6 to 8 servings   Hands-on Time: 10 min.   Total Time: 53 min.

1   cup chopped baked ham
1½ tsp. olive oil
½   (16-oz.) package frozen chopped collard greens, thawed and drained
½   cup diced onion
1½ cups (6 oz.) shredded pepper Jack cheese

1   cup milk
2   large eggs
½   cup all-purpose baking mix
¼   tsp. salt

1. Preheat oven to 400°. Sauté ham in hot oil in a large skillet over medium-high heat 5 minutes or until browned. Stir in collards and onion, and sauté 5 minutes or until onion is tender and liquid evaporates. Layer half of collard mixture in a lightly greased 9-inch pie plate; top with ¾ cup cheese. Repeat layers once.

2. Whisk together milk and remaining ingredients until smooth; pour over collard-and-cheese mixture in pie plate.

3. Bake at 400° for 25 to 35 minutes or until a knife inserted in center comes out clean. Let stand 10 minutes before serving.

Note: We tested with Bisquick All-Purpose Baking Mix.

TO FREEZE IT: Let quiche cool completely. Wrap tightly with aluminum foil; label and freeze up to 1 month. To reheat, preheat oven to 350°. Bake quiche at 350° for 45 minutes.

HAM-AND-CHEESE SANDWICHES

Makes: 8 servings   Hands-on Time: 8 min.   Total Time: 18 min.

Swiss cheese is a perfect choice for these tasty sandwiches because it melts so easily.

¼ cup butter, softened
¼ cup mayonnaise
3 Tbsp. Creole mustard
1 Tbsp. grated onion

2 tsp. poppy seeds
8 hamburger buns, split
1 (6-oz.) package Swiss cheese slices
1 lb. thinly sliced ham

1. Preheat oven to 350°. Combine first 5 ingredients; spread on each bun half. Layer 8 bun halves with cheese and ham; top with remaining halves. Wrap in aluminum foil.

TO FREEZE IT: Freeze labeled foil-wrapped sandwiches up to 1 month. To reheat, bake foil-wrapped, frozen sandwiches at 350° for 1 hour.

2. Bake, in foil, at 350° for 10 minutes or until thoroughly heated.

PANHANDLE SANDWICHES

Makes: 4 servings   Hands-on Time: 15 min.   Total Time: 20 min.

- ½ cup butter, softened
- 4 green onions, diced
- 2 Tbsp. yellow mustard
- 2 tsp. Worcestershire sauce
- 4 (6-inch) French bread loaves, split
- 4 Monterey Jack cheese slices
- 8 deli ham slices

1. Preheat oven to 350°. Stir together first 4 ingredients.

2. Spread butter mixture over cut sides of bread.

3. Cut cheese slices in half; place 2 halves on bottom halves of bread. Top with ham slices and tops of bread. Wrap each sandwich in foil.

TO FREEZE IT: Freeze labeled foil-wrapped sandwiches up to 1 month. To reheat, bake frozen foil-wrapped sandwiches at 350° for 40 minutes.

4. Bake sandwiches at 350° for 5 minutes or until thoroughly heated and cheese melts.

Once you reheat these sandwiches, add additional toppings such as pickles, lettuce, and tomato.

This recipe makes two casseroles so you can serve one now and freeze the other for later. Or freeze both to have on hand for busy weeknights.

CREAMY HAM CASSEROLE

Makes: 2 (4-serving) casseroles   Hands-on Time: 8 min.   Total Time: 38 min.

8   oz. uncooked egg noodles
1   (10¾-oz.) can cream of mushroom soup
1   (8-oz.) container chive-and-onion-flavored cream cheese, softened
⅔   cup milk
2   cups chopped baked glazed ham
1½ cups fresh broccoli florets

1   (9-oz.) package frozen asparagus, thawed
6   baby carrots, chopped
1   (8-oz.) package shredded mozzarella cheese
1   cup (4 oz.) shredded Cheddar cheese
½   cup crushed seasoned croutons

1. Preheat oven to 400°. Cook pasta according to package directions.

2. Stir together soup, cream cheese, and milk in a large bowl. Stir in pasta, ham, and next 3 ingredients. Spoon half of ham mixture into 2 lightly greased 8-inch square baking dishes.

3. Combine cheeses. Sprinkle half of cheese mixture over casseroles. Spoon remaining ham mixture over cheeses.

4. Combine remaining cheese mixture with croutons. Sprinkle over casseroles.

TO FREEZE IT: Wrap casserole in heavy-duty aluminum foil; label and freeze up to 1 month. Thaw frozen casserole in the fridge overnight. Bake, uncovered, at 400° for 35 to 40 minutes.

5. Bake casserole at 400° for 30 minutes or until lightly browned.

make it a meal

Serve this hearty casserole with mixed salad greens and biscuits for a delicious weeknight dinner. Leftover ham works perfectly in this casserole.

This good-for-you soup is even better served with crunchy French bread or cheese toast.

CHUNKY CHICKEN-BARLEY SOUP

Makes: 4 servings (serving size: 1¼ cups)   Hands-on Time: 15 min.   Total Time: 1 hr.

1	cup chopped onion	¼	tsp. salt
1	cup chopped carrot	¼	tsp. dried thyme
½	cup chopped celery	¼	tsp. pepper
2	garlic cloves, minced	1	cup chopped cooked chicken
2	tsp. olive oil	½	cup uncooked quick-cooking barley
2	(14-oz.) cans low-sodium fat-free chicken broth		

1. Sauté first 4 ingredients in hot oil in a large Dutch oven over medium-high heat 5 minutes. Add chicken broth, 1¾ cups water, and next 3 ingredients. Bring to a boil; reduce heat, and simmer, partially covered, 23 to 25 minutes or until vegetables are tender.

2. Add chicken and barley; cook 8 to 10 minutes or until barley is tender.

TO FREEZE IT: Cool soup completely. Freeze meal-size portions in zip-top plastic freezer bags. Seal the bag, removing as much air as possible; label and freeze up to 1 month. To reheat, thaw soup overnight in fridge, and simmer over low heat, stirring occasionally.

CREAMY SLOW-COOKER CHICKEN

Makes: 6 servings   Hands-on Time: 15 min.   Total Time: 4 hr., 15 min.

- 6 skinned and boned chicken breasts (about 2½ lb.)
- 2 tsp. seasoned salt
- 2 Tbsp. canola oil
- 1 (10¾-oz.) can reduced-fat cream of mushroom soup
- 1 (8-oz.) package ⅓-less-fat cream cheese
- ½ cup dry white wine
- 1 (0.7-oz.) envelope Italian dressing mix
- 1 (8-oz.) package sliced fresh mushrooms

Hot cooked rice

1. Sprinkle chicken with seasoned salt. Cook chicken, in batches, in hot oil in a large skillet over medium-high heat 2 to 3 minutes on each side or just until browned. Transfer chicken to a 5-qt. slow cooker, reserving drippings in skillet.

2. Add soup, cream cheese, white wine, and Italian dressing mix to hot drippings in skillet. Cook over medium heat, stirring constantly, 2 to 3 minutes or until cheese is melted and mixture is smooth.

3. Arrange mushrooms over chicken in slow cooker. Spoon soup mixture over mushrooms. Cover and cook on LOW 4 hours. Stir well before serving. Serve over hot cooked rice.

Note: We tested with Good Seasons Italian All Natural Salad Dressing and Recipe Mix.

TO FREEZE IT: Prepare recipe as directed. Transfer to a 13- x 9-inch baking dish, and let cool completely. Label and freeze up to 1 month. To reheat, thaw in fridge 8 to 24 hours. Cover tightly with aluminum foil, and bake at 325° for 45 minutes. Uncover and bake 15 minutes or until thoroughly heated.

Spoon this rich and creamy chicken mixture over pasta, rice, or biscuits for a home-style dinner that's sure to satisfy your need for comfort food.

shortcut secret

To minimize cleanup, buy heavy-duty plastic liners made to fit 3- to 6½-qt. slow cookers. Place the plastic liner inside the slow cooker before adding the recipe ingredients. Then, serve the meal directly from the slow cooker, with the liner in place. Once the cooker has cooled, just toss the plastic liner along with the mess.

ROASTED CHICKEN NOODLE SOUP

Makes: 5 cups   Hands-on Time: 10 min.   Total Time: 30 min.

Turn to this recipe when you have leftover roasted chicken on hand— it takes only 1 cup. Don't worry if you don't have leftovers; a rotisserie chicken from the supermarket deli works just as well.

Vegetable cooking spray
2 cups frozen cubed hash brown potatoes
1½ cups frozen chopped onion, bell pepper, and celery seasoning blend
2 (14-oz.) cans chicken broth

2 oz. wide egg noodles, uncooked (about 1 cup)
¼ tsp. salt
⅛ tsp. dried thyme
1 cup diced roasted chicken breast
1 cup evaporated milk

1. Coat a large saucepan with cooking spray; place over medium-high heat until hot. Add hash brown potatoes and seasoning blend; cook, stirring constantly, 3 minutes.

2. Add broth and next 3 ingredients; bring to a boil. Reduce heat to low, and simmer, partially covered, 7 minutes.

3. Add chicken and milk; cook 5 minutes or until noodles are tender.

TO FREEZE IT: Cook as directed, omitting potatoes. Cool quickly. Freeze in labeled airtight containers, leaving 1-inch headspace, up to 3 months. To reheat, cook frozen soup in a saucepan over medium heat, stirring often, until thoroughly heated. Stir in potatoes, and cook until potatoes are tender.

This classic dish, created and named for 19th-century opera singer Luisa Tetrazzini, is a great way to use leftover cooked chicken. The thin pasta soaks up the sauce, forming a casserole that you can cut with a fork.

CLASSIC CHICKEN TETRAZZINI

Makes: 8 to 10 servings   Hands-on Time: 20 min.   Total Time: 55 min.

1½ (8-oz.) packages vermicelli
½ cup butter
½ cup all-purpose flour
4 cups milk
½ cup dry white wine
2 Tbsp. chicken bouillon granules
1 tsp. seasoned pepper
2 cups freshly grated Parmesan cheese, divided
4 cups diced cooked chicken
1 (6-oz.) jar sliced mushrooms, drained
¾ cup slivered almonds
Garnish: chopped fresh parsley

1. Preheat oven to 350°. Prepare pasta according to package directions.

2. Meanwhile, melt butter in a Dutch oven over low heat; whisk in flour until smooth. Cook 1 minute, whisking constantly. Gradually whisk in milk and wine; cook over medium heat, whisking constantly, 8 to 10 minutes or until mixture is thickened and bubbly. Whisk in bouillon granules, seasoned pepper, and 1 cup Parmesan cheese.

3. Remove from heat; stir in diced cooked chicken, mushrooms, and hot cooked pasta.

4. Spoon mixture into a lightly greased 13- x 9-inch baking dish; sprinkle with slivered almonds and remaining 1 cup Parmesan cheese.

TO FREEZE IT: Label and freeze unbaked casserole up to 1 month. Thaw overnight in fridge. Let stand 30 minutes at room temperature, and bake as directed.

5. Bake at 350° for 35 minutes or until bubbly. Garnish, if desired.

make it a meal

Serve this speedy Italian classic with crusty French bread and mixed salad greens for a fast weeknight supper. It's also great for company.

CHICKEN WITH MUSHROOM SAUCE

Makes: 4 servings   Hands-on Time: 25 min.   Total Time: 57 min.

4	skinned and boned chicken breasts	12	fresh mushrooms, sliced
1½	tsp. salt, divided	4	green onions, chopped
¼	cup all-purpose flour	3	Tbsp. chopped fresh parsley
¼	tsp. pepper	2	Tbsp. capers
½	cup milk	½	cup chicken broth or water
1	cup Italian-seasoned breadcrumbs	½	cup Marsala or white wine
	Olive oil	2	Tbsp. lemon juice
1	garlic clove, minced	2	lemons, sliced

1. Place chicken breasts between 2 sheets of heavy-duty plastic wrap; flatten to ½-inch thickness, using a meat mallet or rolling pin. Sprinkle chicken evenly with ½ tsp. salt.

2. Combine flour, ½ tsp. salt, and pepper in a shallow dish; dredge chicken in flour mixture, shaking off excess. Dip chicken in milk; dredge in breadcrumbs.

3. Pour olive oil to a depth of ¼ inch in a large skillet. Fry chicken, in batches, in hot oil over medium-high heat 5 to 6 minutes on each side. Remove from skillet, and drain on paper towels, reserving 2 Tbsp. drippings in pan.

4. Sauté garlic in hot drippings 20 seconds; add mushrooms, and sauté 3 minutes or until lightly browned. Add green onions, parsley, and capers; sauté 1 minute. Stir in chicken broth, next 3 ingredients, and remaining ½ tsp. salt. Bring to a boil over medium-high heat, and cook, stirring constantly, 2 minutes or until slightly thickened. Serve mushroom sauce over chicken.

TO FREEZE IT: Chicken: Fry as directed until almost done. Cool quickly. Freeze on baking sheets, then place in labeled zip-top plastic freezer bags, and freeze up to 4 months. To reheat, thaw in fridge overnight. Place in a shallow pan, and bake at 350° for 30 to 40 minutes or until temperature reaches 165°. Mushroom Sauce: Ladle room-temperature or chilled sauce into labeled zip-top plastic freezer bags. Seal and freeze for up to 4 months. To reheat, thaw in fridge overnight. Reheat in a medium saucepan over medium heat until thoroughly heated.

CHICKEN ENCHILADAS

Makes: 4 to 6 servings   Hands-on Time: 35 min.   Total Time: 55 min.

2   Tbsp. butter
2   large onions, thinly sliced
2   cups chopped cooked chicken
½   cup diced roasted red bell pepper
2   (3-oz.) packages cream cheese, cubed
¼   tsp. salt
¼   tsp. pepper
4   (4.5-oz.) cans diced green chiles
1   small onion, chopped
2   garlic cloves, minced
2   tsp. dried oregano
1   tsp. ground cumin
½   tsp. sugar
1   (14-oz.) can chicken broth
½   cup salsa
10 (7-inch) flour tortillas
2   cups (8 oz.) shredded Cheddar cheese
Garnishes: shredded romaine lettuce, chopped tomato

These easy, cheesy chicken enchiladas come together in a snap. Double the recipe and have one now; share the other one with a time-starved friend.

1. Preheat oven to 375°. Melt butter in a large skillet over medium-high heat, stirring often; add sliced onions, and cook 15 minutes or until caramelized. Reduce heat to low, and add chicken and next 4 ingredients, stirring until combined. Set aside. Pulse chiles and next 5 ingredients in blender or food processor several times until combined.

2. Bring chile mixture and chicken broth to a boil in a saucepan over high heat; cook 5 minutes or until slightly thickened. (Mixture should be the consistency of a thin gravy.) Remove from heat, and stir in salsa.

3. Spread one-third chile mixture on bottom of a lightly greased 13- x 9-inch baking dish.

TO FREEZE IT: Freeze chile mixture and filled tortillas separately in labeled airtight containers up to 1 month, if desired. To reheat, thaw in fridge overnight. Prepare and bake as directed.

4. Spoon chicken mixture down center of each tortilla; roll up, and place seam side down in prepared baking dish. Top with remaining chile mixture; sprinkle with cheese.

5. Bake at 375° for 20 to 25 minutes or until bubbly. Garnish, if desired.

test kitchen tip

To lighten, substitute ⅓-less-fat cream cheese, 2% reduced-fat Cheddar cheese, and fat-free tortillas.

LESLIE'S FAVORITE CHICKEN-AND-WILD RICE CASSEROLE

Makes: 6 to 8 servings   Hands-on Time: 40 min.   Total Time: 1 hr., 15 min.

This recipe cuts preparation time by using convenience products. Make one large casserole, or divide it between two smaller baking pans.

2   (6.2-oz.) boxes fast-cooking long-grain and wild rice mix
¼   cup butter
4   celery ribs, chopped
2   medium onions, chopped
2   (8-oz.) cans sliced water chestnuts, drained
5   cups chopped cooked chicken
3   cups (12 oz.) shredded Cheddar cheese, divided

2   (10¾-oz.) cans cream of mushroom soup
1   (16-oz.) container sour cream
1   cup milk
½   tsp. salt
½   tsp. pepper
2   cups soft, fresh breadcrumbs
1   (2.25-oz.) package sliced almonds, toasted

1. Preheat oven to 350°. Prepare rice mixes according to package directions.

2. Meanwhile, melt butter in a large skillet over medium heat; add celery and onion. Sauté 10 minutes or until tender.

3. Combine water chestnuts, cooked rice, celery mixture, chicken, cheese, and next 5 ingredients in a very large bowl.

4. Spoon mixture into a lightly greased 15- x 10-inch baking dish or a 4-qt. baking dish. Top casserole with breadcrumbs.

TO FREEZE IT: You can divide this casserole between 2 (11- x 7-inch) baking dishes. Label and freeze unbaked casserole up to 1 month. To heat, remove from freezer, and let stand at room temperature 1 hour. Bake, covered, at 350° for 30 minutes. Uncover casserole, and bake 55 more minutes. Sprinkle with almonds.

5. Bake, uncovered, at 350° for 35 minutes. Sprinkle with almonds.

ANYTIME CHICKEN AND DRESSING

Makes: 6 servings   Hands-on Time: 25 min.   Total Time: 1 hr., 10 min.

- ¼ cup butter
- 7 green onions, chopped
- 2 celery ribs, chopped
- 10 cornbread muffins, crumbled (about 3½ cups)
- ½ (16-oz.) package herb-seasoned stuffing mix
- 5 cups chicken broth
- 1½ cups chopped cooked chicken
- 2 large eggs, lightly beaten
- ½ tsp. poultry seasoning

1. Preheat oven to 350°. Melt butter in a large skillet over medium heat; add green onions and celery, and sauté 5 minutes or until tender.

2. Combine cornbread and remaining ingredients in a large bowl; add sautéed vegetable mixture, stirring well. Spoon dressing into a lightly greased 13- x 9-inch baking dish.

TO FREEZE IT: Cover baking dish tightly with heavy-duty aluminum foil; label and freeze up to 2 months. To heat, let casserole thaw overnight in fridge. Uncover and bake at 350° for 55 minutes or until lightly browned.

3. Bake, uncovered, at 350° for 45 minutes or until lightly browned.

You can either make or purchase cornbread that's to your liking for this recipe. We prefer cornbread that's not so sweet.

make it a meal

Sweet potato fries are easy, nutritious, and make a perfect complement to this dish. Peel sweet potatoes, and cut into ¼-inch strips. Toss with just enough oil to coat, and arrange in a single layer on a baking sheet coated with cooking spray. Bake at 425° for 20 minutes or until edges are lightly browned.

EASY CHICKEN AND DUMPLINGS

Makes: 4 to 6 servings   Hands-on Time: 30 min.   Total Time: 40 min.

Deli-roasted chicken, cream of chicken soup, and canned biscuits make a quick-and-tasty version of this Southern favorite.

1   (32-oz.) container low-sodium chicken broth
3   cups shredded cooked chicken (about 1½ lb.)
1   (10¾-oz.) can reduced-fat cream of chicken soup
¼   tsp. poultry seasoning

1   (10-oz.) can refrigerated jumbo buttermilk biscuits
3   celery ribs, diced
2   carrots, diced
Salt and freshly ground black pepper to taste

1. Bring first 4 ingredients to a boil in a Dutch oven over medium-high heat. Cover, reduce heat to low, and simmer, stirring occasionally, 5 minutes. Increase heat to medium-high; return to a low boil.

2. Place biscuits on a lightly floured surface. Roll or pat each biscuit to ⅛-inch thickness; cut into ½-inch-wide strips.

3. Drop strips, 1 at a time, into boiling broth mixture. Add celery and carrots. Cover, reduce heat to low, and simmer 15 to 20 minutes, stirring occasionally to prevent dumplings from sticking. Season to taste with salt and pepper.

TO FREEZE IT: Quickly cool chicken and dumplings, and place in a labeled airtight container. Freeze up to 1 month. To reheat, heat frozen chicken and dumplings to simmer over low heat, stirring occasionally.

TORTILLA SOUP

Makes: 22 cups   Hands-on Time: 57 min.   Total Time: 2 hr., 32 min.

Mesquite chips

8   skinned and boned chicken breasts

16 medium tomatoes (about 8½ lb.)

2   large onions, peeled and cut into eighths

1   Tbsp. vegetable oil

2   poblano peppers

3   garlic cloves, minced

2   (10-oz.) packages 6-inch corn tortillas, cut into thin strips and divided

5   (14-oz.) cans chicken broth

4   (14-oz.) cans beef broth

1   (8-oz.) can tomato sauce

1   Tbsp. ground cumin

1   Tbsp. chili powder

1   bay leaf

½   tsp. salt

½   tsp. ground red pepper

½   cup vegetable oil

2   cups (8 oz.) shredded colby-Jack cheese blend

1   avocado, peeled and diced

Garnishes: fresh cilantro, lime wedges

1. Preheat grill to 350° to 400° (medium-high) heat. Wrap mesquite chips in heavy-duty aluminum foil; punch holes in top of foil. (Soak chips in water 1 hour, then drain if using charcoal grill.) Place on coals.

2. Grill chicken, covered with grill lid, 6 minutes on each side or until done. Remove chicken; chop and set aside.

3. Place tomatoes and onion on a large piece of heavy-duty aluminum foil. Brush with 1 Tbsp. oil; fold foil to seal. Place on cooking grate. Grill, covered, 10 minutes. Place poblano peppers on cooking grate with foil-wrapped vegetables, and grill, covered, 10 minutes.

4. Peel peppers, remove seeds, and chop.

5. Process one-third tomato mixture in a food processor until smooth. Press through a wire-mesh strainer into a bowl, discarding solids; transfer to a Dutch oven. Repeat procedure twice with remaining tomato mixture. Stir in chopped peppers and garlic.

6. Add half of tortilla strips and next 8 ingredients to tomato mixture. Bring to a boil. Cover, reduce heat, and simmer 30 minutes. Stir in chicken. Discard bay leaf.

TO FREEZE IT: Cool soup completely. Freeze in a labeled airtight container up to 3 months. To reheat, thaw soup overnight in fridge, and simmer over low heat, stirring occasionally.

7. Pour ½ cup oil into a large skillet. Fry remaining tortilla strips in hot oil until crisp. Drain on paper towels.

8. Top servings with crisp tortilla strips, cheese, and avocado. Garnish, if desired.

CAJUN SHRIMP CASSEROLE

Makes: 6 servings   Hands-on Time: 30 min.   Total Time: 1 hr., 6 min.

This longer ingredient list is worth the effort for a special-occasion meal. If you're not a fan of okra, it's okay to leave it out of this dish.

2 lb. unpeeled, large raw shrimp	1½ tsp. salt
¼ cup butter	3 cups cooked long-grain rice
1 small red onion, chopped*	1 (10¾-oz.) can cream of shrimp soup**
½ cup chopped red bell pepper*	½ cup dry white wine
½ cup chopped yellow bell pepper*	1 Tbsp. soy sauce
½ cup chopped green bell pepper*	½ tsp. ground red pepper
4 garlic cloves, minced	¼ cup grated Parmesan cheese
2 cups fresh or frozen sliced okra	
1 Tbsp. lemon juice	

1. Preheat oven to 350°. Peel shrimp; devein, if desired.

2. Melt butter in a large skillet over medium-high heat. Add onion and next 3 ingredients; sauté 7 minutes or until tender. Add garlic, and sauté 1 minute. Stir in okra, lemon juice, and salt; sauté 5 minutes. Add shrimp, and cook 3 minutes or until shrimp turn pink. Stir in rice and next 4 ingredients until blended. Pour into a lightly greased 11- x 7-inch baking dish.

TO FREEZE IT: Cover tightly, label, and freeze unbaked casserole, omitting Parmesan cheese and garnishes. To prepare, remove from freezer, and let stand at room temperature 30 minutes before baking. Bake, covered, at 350° for 50 minutes. Uncover; sprinkle with Parmesan cheese, and bake 10 more minutes or until cheese is lightly browned.

3. Sprinkle with Parmesan cheese. Bake at 350° for 15 to 20 minutes or until casserole is bubbly and cheese is lightly browned.

*1 (10-oz.) package frozen chopped onions and peppers may be substituted for fresh onion and bell peppers.

**1 (10¾-oz.) can cream of mushroom soup may be substituted for cream of shrimp soup.

CRAWFISH ÉTOUFFÉE

Makes: 6 servings   Hands-on Time: 41 min.   Total Time: 41 min.

- 1   cup uncooked long-grain rice
- ¼   cup butter
- 1   large onion, chopped
- 1   green bell pepper, chopped
- 4   celery ribs, chopped (about 1 cup)
- 4   garlic cloves, minced
- 1   (10¾-oz.) can cream of mushroom soup
- 1   (14-oz.) can chicken broth
- 1   Tbsp. salt-free Cajun seasoning
- ⅛   to ¼ tsp. ground red pepper
- 1   lb. frozen cooked peeled crawfish tails, thawed and drained
- ¼   cup chopped green onions
- 3   Tbsp. chopped fresh parsley
- ¼   tsp. freshly ground black pepper

1. Prepare rice according to package directions.

2. Melt butter in a large cast-iron skillet or Dutch oven over medium heat. Add onion and next 3 ingredients; cook, stirring constantly, 8 minutes.

3. Stir together soup and chicken broth. Add to vegetable mixture. Stir in Cajun seasoning and ground red pepper.

4. Cook over medium-low heat 10 minutes, stirring occasionally. Stir in crawfish, green onions, and parsley; cook 3 minutes or until hot. Serve over rice. Sprinkle with black pepper.

TO FREEZE IT: Divide étouffée into 3 (1-qt.) zip-top plastic freezer bags. Label and freeze up to 1 month. To reheat, thaw in fridge overnight. Remove from freezer bag, and cook in a saucepan over medium-low heat, stirring until thoroughly heated. Each bag contains about 2 servings.

> You can forgo the roux in this quick étouffée by stirring in a can of cream of mushroom soup as a thickener.

shortcut secret

You can purchase frozen, cooked, peeled crawfish tails in the freezer section of your grocery store. We prefer Louisiana crawfish tails.

The sauce starts with a roux. Be sure to get into the corners of the pan when you stir so the flour there doesn't scorch.

CREOLE SHRIMP AND GRITS

Makes: 6 to 8 servings   Hands-on Time: 30 min.   Total Time: 2 hr., 2 min.

2 lb. unpeeled, medium-size raw shrimp	1 bay leaf
¼ cup vegetable oil	1½ tsp. Creole seasoning
⅓ cup all-purpose flour	1 tsp. lemon juice
1 medium onion, finely chopped	½ tsp. Worcestershire sauce
2 celery ribs, chopped	2½ cups milk
1 medium-size green bell pepper, chopped	1 tsp. salt
2 garlic cloves, chopped	1½ cups uncooked quick-cooking grits
1 (6-oz.) can tomato paste	Garnish: celery leaves

1. Peel shrimp, reserving shells; devein shrimp, if desired. Bring shells and 4 cups water to a boil in a medium saucepan over medium-high heat; reduce heat to low, and cook 20 minutes. Pour shrimp broth through a wire-mesh strainer into a large bowl, pressing shells with back of a spoon; discard shells.

2. Heat oil in a Dutch oven over medium heat; stir in flour, and cook, stirring constantly, until flour is caramel colored (about 8 to 10 minutes). Add onion and next 3 ingredients, and cook, stirring often, 5 to 7 minutes or until tender. Stir in 2 cups shrimp broth, tomato paste, and next 4 ingredients. Reduce heat to low, and cook, stirring occasionally, 45 minutes. Add shrimp, and cook 10 minutes, stirring in ¼ to ½ cup remaining shrimp broth to reach desired consistency.

3. Meanwhile, bring milk, 2½ cups water, and salt to a boil in a saucepan over high heat. Gradually stir in grits. Reduce heat to low, and simmer, stirring occasionally, 10 to 12 minutes or until thickened. Discard bay leaf. Serve Creole Shrimp over grits. Garnish, if desired.

TO FREEZE IT: Divide shrimp mixture between 2 labeled (1-gallon) freezer bags. Lay flat on a baking sheet in freezer. Once frozen, remove baking sheet from freezer. To reheat, thaw in fridge overnight. Reheat over medium-low, stirring occasionally, 15 minutes.

crowd pleasers

SPICY WHITE CHEESE DIP

Makes: about 8 cups   Hands-on Time: 10 min.   Total Time: 3 hr., 10 min.

This crowd pleaser gets its kick from canned diced tomatoes and green chiles.

2 lb. white American deli cheese slices, torn
1 small onion, finely chopped
1 tsp. jarred minced garlic
2 (10-oz.) cans diced tomatoes and green chiles
¾ cup milk
½ tsp. ground cumin
½ tsp. coarsely ground pepper
1 jalapeño pepper, chopped (optional)
Assorted chips, lime wedges

1. Place all ingredients except jalapeño, chips, and lime wedges in a 6-qt. slow cooker. Cover and cook on LOW 3 hours, stirring gently every hour. Stir before serving. Turn slow cooker to WARM. Sprinkle with jalapeños, if desired. Serve with chips and lime wedges.

TO FREEZE IT: Spoon into labeled quart-size freezer containers; freeze up to 1 month. Thaw in fridge overnight. Microwave at HIGH, stirring at 1-minute intervals, until thoroughly heated.

shortcut secret

Buy white American cheese by the pound at the deli counter to make this addictive dip. Have the cheese sliced at the deli; then just roughly tear the slices, and place them in the slow cooker.

INCREDIBLE PIMIENTO CHEESE

Makes: 8 cups   Hands-on Time: 10 min.   Total Time: 10 min.

- 2 (8-oz.) packages Cheddar cheese
- 2 (8-oz.) packages sharp Cheddar cheese
- 1 (16-oz.) package prepared cheese product
- 3 Tbsp. sugar
- ½ tsp. salt
- ½ tsp. pepper
- 2 (4-oz.) jars diced pimiento, drained
- 2 cups mayonnaise

1. Position shredding disk in food processor bowl; shred Cheddar cheeses. Cut cheese loaf into cubes. Position knife blade in processor bowl; add half of cheeses. Process until smooth, stopping once to scrape down sides. Transfer mixture to a bowl.

2. Add remaining cheeses, sugar, salt, and pepper to processor bowl; process until smooth, stopping once to scrape down sides.

3. Stir into cheese mixture in bowl. Stir in pimiento and mayonnaise.

TO FREEZE IT: Wrap pimiento cheese tightly with plastic wrap, and place in a labeled airtight container. Freeze up to 1 month. Thaw in fridge overnight.

You can also use a box grater to achieve coarsely grated and finely shredded Cheddar cheese.

BAKED GOAT CHEESE DIP

Makes: 12 servings   Hands-on Time: 20 min.   Total Time: 35 min.

1   small onion, diced
1   Tbsp. olive oil
2   garlic cloves, minced
2   Tbsp. tomato paste
¼   tsp. dried crushed red pepper
Pinch of sugar
1   (14.5-oz.) can petite diced tomatoes
¼   cup chopped sun-dried tomatoes
    in oil

¼   cup torn basil leaves
Salt and pepper to taste
2   (4-oz.) goat cheese logs, softened
1   (8-oz.) package cream cheese,
    softened
Assorted cut vegetables, bread
    cubes

1. Preheat oven to 350°. Sauté onion in hot oil in a 3-qt. saucepan over medium-high heat 5 minutes or until tender. Stir in garlic and next 3 ingredients, and cook, stirring constantly, 1 minute. Stir in diced and sun-dried tomatoes. Reduce heat to medium-low, and simmer, stirring occasionally, 10 minutes or until very thick. Remove from heat, and stir in basil and salt and pepper to taste.

2. Stir together goat cheese and cream cheese until well blended. Spread into a lightly greased 9-inch shallow ovenproof dish. Top with tomato mixture.

TO FREEZE IT: Prepare recipe as directed through Step 2. Cover, label, and freeze up to 1 month. Thaw in fridge overnight. Let stand at room temperature 30 minutes. Bake as directed.

3. Bake at 350° for 15 to 18 minutes or until thoroughly heated. Serve with assorted vegetables and bread cubes.

The rich and salty flavor of the feta cheese will make this Greek-inspired appetizer a huge hit among your guests.

FETA CHEESE SQUARES

Makes: 5 dozen   Hands-on Time: 10 min.   Total Time: 50 min.

2   cups all-purpose baking mix
1½ tsp. baking powder
¼   tsp. salt
1   cup milk
½   cup butter, melted

4   (4-oz.) packages feta cheese with garlic and herbs, crumbled
1   (8-oz.) container small-curd cottage cheese
3   large eggs, lightly beaten

1. Preheat oven to 350°. Stir together baking mix, baking powder, and salt in a large bowl. Stir in milk and remaining ingredients, stirring just until dry ingredients are moistened. Spoon cheese mixture into a lightly greased 15- x 10-inch jelly-roll pan.

2. Bake at 350° for 30 minutes or until golden brown and set. Remove from oven, and let cool on a wire rack 10 minutes. Cut into 1½-inch squares, and serve immediately.

Note: We tested with Bisquick All-Purpose Baking Mix.

TO FREEZE IT: Bake as directed, and freeze in a labeled airtight container or zip-top plastic freezer bag up to 1 month. Preheat oven to 350°, and bake frozen squares on a baking sheet for 10 to 15 minutes or until thoroughly heated.

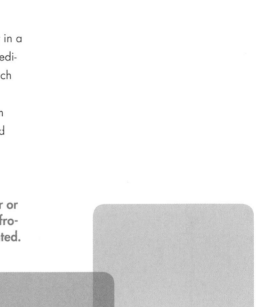

FIG-AND-GRUYÈRE PASTRIES

Makes: 56 appetizers   Hands-on Time: 10 min.   Total Time: 34 min.

1   (17.3-oz.) package frozen puff
    pastry sheets, thawed
2   cups (8 oz.) shredded Gruyère
    cheese, divided

½   cup fig preserves, melted

1. Preheat oven to 400°. Roll 1 puff pastry sheet into a 14- x 10-inch rectangle. Sprinkle with 1 cup Gruyère cheese. Roll in both narrow ends of puff pastry sheet to meet in center of rectangle. Repeat procedure with remaining puff pastry sheet and Gruyère cheese.

TO FREEZE IT: Wrap uncut rolls in heavy-duty plastic wrap, label, and freeze. To prepare, let rolls stand at room temperature 10 minutes before slicing. Brush with preserves, and bake as directed.

2. Cut each roll into ¼-inch slices. Place slices on parchment paper-lined baking sheets; brush with melted preserves. Bake at 400° for 12 minutes or until golden. Serve warm.

Fig preserves and Swiss-made Gruyère cheese pair well in this classic French pastry sometimes called a palmier (pahlm-YAY). They are first cousins to the elephant ears sold at carnivals. A light and slightly sweet Riesling or Gewürztraminer is your best bet with these.

Freshly shredded cheese is a must for these sausage balls, which have become a traditional favorite during the holidays. The three-ingredient recipe is the perfect finger food for Christmas morning when children are too excited to sit down for breakfast. Serve with wedges of fresh red and green apples and pears.

SAUSAGE BALLS

Makes: about 8 dozen   Hands-on Time: 30 min.   Total Time: 1 hr., 30 min.

3   cups all-purpose baking mix
1   lb. ground hot pork sausage

1   (10-oz.) package sharp
    Cheddar cheese, shredded

1. Preheat oven to 350°. Combine all ingredients in a large bowl, pressing mixture together with hands. Shape into ¾-inch balls, and place on lightly greased baking sheets.

TO FREEZE IT: Freeze uncooked Sausage Balls in a labeled airtight container up to 2 months. Thaw in fridge overnight. Preheat oven to 400°. Bake frozen balls for 18 to 20 minutes or until lightly browned.

2. Bake at 350° for 15 to 18 minutes or until lightly browned.

Note: We tested with Bisquick All-Purpose Baking Mix and Cracker Barrel Sharp Cheddar Cheese.

TACO TEASERS

Makes: 40 appetizer servings
Hands-on Time: 10 min.   Total Time: 3 hr., 34 min., including mayonnaise

1 lb. ground beef	40 won ton wrappers
1 small onion, chopped	Vegetable oil
¼ cup chopped green bell pepper	Tex-Mex Mayonnaise or sour cream
1 (1¼-oz.) envelope taco seasoning mix	and salsa
1 cup (4 oz.) shredded Monterey Jack or Cheddar cheese	

1. Brown first 3 ingredients in a large nonstick skillet, stirring until beef crumbles and is no longer pink. Drain and return beef mixture to skillet. Add ¼ cup water and taco seasoning.

2. Simmer 3 to 4 minutes or until liquid evaporates. Remove from heat, and stir in cheese.

3. Spoon 1 level Tbsp. of mixture onto center of each won ton wrapper.

4. Moisten won ton wrapper edges with water. Bring corners together, pressing to seal.

TO FREEZE IT: Store uncooked appetizers in a labeled airtight container in freezer up to 1 month. Fry, unthawed, in hot oil 2½ minutes on each side or until golden.

5. Pour oil to a depth of 2 inches in a Dutch oven; heat to 365°. Fry filled won tons, in batches, 2 minutes on each side or until golden. Drain on wire racks over paper towels. Serve with Tex-Mex Mayonnaise.

Tex-Mex mayonnaise

Makes: 1¼ cups   Hands-on Time: 8 min.   Total Time: 3 hr., 8 min.

A dollop of this mayonnaise adds zesty flavor to sandwiches, raw vegetables, or even grilled burgers.

1 cup mayonnaise	½ tsp. onion powder
2 Tbsp. ketchup	½ tsp. garlic powder
2 Tbsp. lime juice	½ tsp. hot sauce
2 Tbsp. milk	½ tsp. Worcestershire sauce
2 to 3 tsp. chili powder	¼ tsp. lemon pepper
1 tsp. ground red pepper	

1. Combine all ingredients in a bowl. Cover and chill at least 3 hours.

MILD

Taco
Seasoning Mix

Serving
Suggestion

(28g)

These spinach-and-artichoke appetizers only look difficult to make. The secret is puff pastry. Simply spread the filling over the pastry, slice, and bake.

SPINACH AND ARTICHOKES IN PUFF PASTRY

Makes: 4 dozen   Hands-on Time: 20 min.   Total Time: 1 hr., 40 min.

- 1 (10-oz.) package frozen chopped spinach, thawed
- 1 (14-oz.) can artichoke hearts, drained and chopped
- ½ cup mayonnaise
- ½ cup grated Parmesan cheese
- 1 tsp. onion powder
- 1 tsp. garlic powder
- ½ tsp. pepper
- 1 (17.3-oz.) package frozen puff pastry sheets

1. Drain spinach well, pressing between layers of paper towels.

2. Stir together spinach, artichoke hearts, and next 5 ingredients.

3. Thaw puff pastry at room temperature 30 minutes. Unfold pastry, and place on a lightly floured surface or heavy-duty plastic wrap. Spread half of spinach mixture over pastry sheet, leaving a ½-inch border. Roll up pastry, jelly-roll fashion, pressing to seal seam; wrap in heavy-duty plastic wrap. Repeat procedure with remaining pastry and spinach mixture. Freeze 30 minutes.

TO FREEZE IT: Label pastry. Rolled pastry may remain in freezer up to 3 months.

4. Preheat oven to 400°. Cut rolled pastry into ½-inch-thick slices. Bake at 400° for 20 minutes or until golden brown.

HAM-AND-CHEESE TARTLETS

Makes: 18 tartlets   Hands-on Time: 20 min.   Total Time: 1 hr.

3   (10-oz.) packages frozen pastry
     shells
2¼ cups (9 oz.) shredded Cheddar
     cheese

3   Tbsp. all-purpose flour
3   large eggs
1   cup whipping cream
1½ cups diced cooked ham

1. Preheat oven to 325°. Place pastry shells on a baking sheet. Bake at 325° for 20 minutes or until lightly browned. Remove tops. Stir together cheese and flour.

2. Whisk together eggs and whipping cream; stir in cheese mixture and diced ham. Spoon mixture into prepared pastry shells.

3. Bake at 325° for 20 minutes or until golden brown.

TO FREEZE IT: Freeze baked tartlets in a labeled airtight container up to 1 month. Thaw and bake tartlets at 325° for 10 minutes or until thoroughly heated.

Get the party started! These flaky and tender bites make the perfect appetizers for cocktail parties.

CHEESE PUFFS

Makes: 5¼ dozen   Hands-on Time: 40 min.   Total Time: 55 min.

2   large eggs
1   (3-oz.) package cream
     cheese, softened
¼   cup cottage cheese

4   oz. feta cheese
1   (16-oz.) package frozen
     phyllo pastry, thawed
Unsalted butter, melted

1. Preheat oven to 375°. Beat eggs at medium speed with an electric mixer 1 minute; beat in cheeses.

2. Unfold phyllo, and cover with a slightly damp towel to prevent pastry from drying out.

3. Place 1 phyllo sheet on a flat surface covered with wax paper; cut lengthwise into 3 (12- x 6-inch) strips. Brush 1 long side of each strip with melted butter; fold strips in half lengthwise, and brush with butter.

4. Place 1 tsp. cheese mixture at base of each strip; fold right bottom corner over to form a triangle. Continue folding back and forth into a triangle, gently pressing corners together.

5. Place triangles, seam side down, on ungreased baking sheets, and brush with butter. Repeat procedure with remaining phyllo sheets, cheese mixture, and butter.

TO FREEZE IT: Freeze unbaked pastries on baking sheets; remove to labeled airtight containers, and freeze up to 2 weeks. Bake as directed without thawing.

6. Bake at 375° for 15 minutes or until golden.

In addition to making a perfect appetizer, these rich favorites fill in as a hearty breakfast. Keep them handy in the freezer.

SPINACH QUICHES

Makes: 4 dozen   Hands-on Time: 25 min.   Total Time: 1 hr.

1   (14.1-oz.) package refrigerated piecrusts
2   Tbsp. butter
1   small onion, chopped
2   green onions, chopped
¼   cup chopped fresh parsley
1   (10-oz.) package frozen chopped spinach, thawed and well drained

1   Tbsp. Worcestershire sauce
1   tsp. salt
½   tsp. pepper
3   large eggs
¼   cup milk
1   cup (4 oz.) shredded Swiss cheese

1. Preheat oven to 350°. Roll each piecrust into a 12-inch square; cut each square into 24 pieces. Shape into balls, and press into lightly greased miniature muffin pans.

2. Melt butter in a large skillet over medium heat. Add onions and parsley; sauté until onions are tender. Add spinach; cook 2 minutes. Stir in Worcestershire sauce, salt, and pepper. Remove from heat.

3. Whisk together eggs and milk until blended; stir in cheese. Add egg mixture to spinach mixture; spoon into prepared pans.

4. Bake at 350° for 30 to 35 minutes. Remove immediately from pans, and cool on wire racks.

TO FREEZE IT: Place baked quiches in labeled airtight containers in the freezer up to 2 months. Thaw frozen quiches in the fridge overnight; bake at 300° for 10 minutes or until thoroughly heated.

Generous layers of corned beef, Swiss cheese, and sauerkraut nestled between rye bread make up the Reuben sandwich, a classic deli staple. This is the perfect sandwich to serve when the guys are coming over to watch sports. So keep a batch in the freezer for an easy, last-minute gathering.

GOLDEN-BAKED MINI REUBENS

Makes: 20 sandwiches   Hands-on Time: 20 min.   Total Time: 30 min.

½ cup Thousand Island dressing
1 (16-oz.) loaf party rye bread
1 (6-oz.) package Swiss cheese slices, halved

12 oz. thinly sliced corned beef
1 (16-oz.) can shredded sauerkraut, well drained
Butter-flavored cooking spray

1. Preheat oven to 375°. Spread dressing on 1 side of each bread slice; top half of slices with half of cheese, corned beef, sauerkraut, and remaining cheese. Top with remaining bread slices.

2. Coat a baking sheet with cooking spray; arrange sandwiches on baking sheet. Coat bottom of a second baking sheet with cooking spray; place, coated side down, on sandwiches.

TO FREEZE IT: Place unbaked sandwiches on baking sheets, and freeze until firm; place sandwiches in a labeled heavy-duty zip-top plastic freezer bags, and freeze up to 1 month. Preheat oven to 375°, and bake for 15 minutes or until bread is golden and cheese melts.

3. Bake at 375° for 8 to 10 minutes or until bread is golden and cheese melts.

test kitchen tip

The secret to making a delicious Reuben sandwich is to be certain to thoroughly drain the sauerkraut. Otherwise, the sandwich becomes soggy, and won't be as tasty when it comes out of the freezer.

Get a jump on holiday parties. Plan to stash a few batches of these casual three-bite sandwiches in your freezer. This roast beef sandwich recipe is easy for family gatherings as well as upscale entertaining events.

HOT ROAST BEEF PARTY SANDWICHES

Makes: 12 to 16 servings   Hands-on Time: 26 min.   Total Time: 56 min.

½   cup finely chopped walnuts
2   (9.25-oz.) packages dinner rolls
⅔   cup peach preserves
½   cup mustard-mayonnaise blend

¾   lb. thinly sliced deli roast beef, chopped
½   lb. thinly sliced Havarti cheese
Salt and pepper (optional)

1. Preheat oven to 325°.

2. Heat walnuts in a small nonstick skillet over medium-low heat, stirring often, 5 to 6 minutes or until lightly toasted and fragrant.

3. Remove rolls from packages. (Do not separate rolls.) Cut rolls in half horizontally, creating 1 top and 1 bottom per package. Spread preserves on cut sides of top of rolls; sprinkle with walnuts. Spread mustard-mayonnaise blend on cut sides of bottom of rolls; top with roast beef and cheese. Sprinkle with salt and pepper, if desired. Cover with top halves of rolls, preserves sides down, and wrap in aluminum foil.

TO FREEZE IT: Prepare recipe as directed through Step 3, label, and freeze up to 1 month. Thaw in fridge overnight, and bake as directed in Step 4.

4. Bake at 325° for 30 minutes or until cheese is melted. Slice into individual sandwiches. Serve immediately.

Note: We tested with Rainbo Dinner Time Rolls, Hellmann's Dijonnaise Creamy Dijon Mustard, and Boar's Head Londonport Roast Beef.

Southern cooking perfection, these tasty treats take the best of breakfast—grits, bacon, and sharp Cheddar cheese—and re-create them as scrumptious fried balls. Serve with hot sauce, if desired.

BACON-GRITS FRITTERS

Makes: about 32   Hands-on Time: 35 min.   Total Time: 4 hr., 40 min.

1   cup uncooked quick-cooking grits
4   cups milk
1   tsp. salt
1½   cups (6 oz.) shredded extra-sharp white Cheddar cheese
½   cup cooked and finely crumbled bacon (about 8 slices)
2   green onions, minced
½   tsp. freshly ground pepper
2   large eggs
3   cups Japanese breadcrumbs (panko)
Vegetable oil

1. Prepare grits according to package directions, using 4 cups milk and 1 tsp. salt. Remove from heat, and let stand 5 minutes. Stir in cheese and next 3 ingredients, stirring until cheese is melted. Spoon mixture into a lightly greased 8-inch square baking dish or pan, and chill 4 to 24 hours.

2. Roll grits into 1½-inch balls. Whisk together eggs and ¼ cup water. Dip balls in egg wash, and roll in breadcrumbs.

TO FREEZE IT: Prepare recipe as directed through Step 2, and freeze on a baking sheet for 30 minutes or until firm. Transfer to a labeled zip-top plastic freezer bag, and freeze. Cook frozen fritters as directed in Step 3, increasing cooking time to 5 to 6 minutes or until golden and centers are thoroughly heated.

3. Pour oil to depth of 3 inches in a large heavy skillet; heat over medium-high heat to 350°. Fry fritters, in batches, 3 to 4 minutes or until golden brown. Drain on paper towels. Keep fritters warm on a wire rack in a jelly-roll pan in a 225° oven up to 30 minutes. Serve warm.

Serve these great dippers with store-bought pizza sauce, or freeze ahead the Zesty Pizza Sauce on page 20.

PARMESAN TWISTS

Makes: 4 dozen   Hands-on Time: 20 min.   Total Time: 1 hr., 5 min.

½   cup butter, softened
1   cup shredded Parmesan cheese
1   (8-oz.) container sour cream
2   cups all-purpose flour

2   tsp. dried Italian seasoning
1   egg yolk
2   Tbsp. sesame seeds

1. Preheat oven to 350°. Beat butter at medium speed with an electric mixer until fluffy. Add cheese and sour cream, beating until blended.

2. Combine flour and Italian seasoning. Gradually add to butter mixture; beat at low speed until blended. Cover and chill 30 minutes.

3. Turn dough out onto a lightly floured surface; knead 3 or 4 times. Divide dough in half. Roll half of dough into a 12- x 6-inch rectangle. Cut into 6- x ½-inch strips. Stir together egg yolk and 1 Tbsp. water; brush over breadsticks. Sprinkle with 1 Tbsp. sesame seeds. Twist strips, and place on lightly greased baking sheets. Repeat with remaining dough, egg wash, and sesame seeds.

4. Bake at 350° for 15 minutes or until golden.

TO FREEZE IT: Place baked Parmesan Twists in a labeled airtight container, and freeze up to 6 months. Thaw at room temperature, and reheat at 350° for 5 minutes.

HURRY-UP HOMEMADE CRESCENT ROLLS

Makes: 1 dozen   Hands-on Time: 25 min.   Total Time: 1 hr., 40 min.

This from-scratch recipe is suited for any level of cook—even first timers. They're perfect for holiday entertaining or gift giving.

1   (¼-oz.) envelope active dry yeast
¾   cup warm water (100° to 110°)
3   to 3½ cups all-purpose baking mix

2   Tbsp. sugar
     All-purpose flour

1. Combine yeast and warm water in a 1-cup measuring cup; let stand 5 minutes. Combine 3 cups baking mix and sugar in a large bowl; gradually stir in yeast mixture.

2. Turn dough out onto a floured surface, and knead, adding additional baking mix (up to ½ cup) as needed, until dough is smooth and elastic (about 10 minutes).

3. Roll dough into a 12-inch circle; cut circle into 12 wedges. Roll up wedges, starting at wide end, to form a crescent shape; place point sides down on a lightly greased baking sheet. Cover and let rise in a warm place (85°), free from drafts, 1 hour or until doubled in bulk.

TO FREEZE IT: Bake rolls at 425° for 5 minutes; cool completely (about 30 minutes). Wrap in aluminum foil, label, and freeze in an airtight container up to 2 months. Thaw at room temperature on a lightly greased baking sheet; bake at 425° for 7 to 8 minutes or until golden.

4. Preheat oven to 425°. Bake 10 to 12 minutes or until golden.

Note: We tested with Bisquick All-Purpose Baking Mix.

test kitchen tip

To make rolls in a heavy-duty electric stand mixer, prepare as directed in Step 1. Using dough hook attachment, beat dough at medium speed about 5 minutes, beating in ½ cup additional baking mix, if needed, until dough leaves the sides of the bowl and pulls together, becoming soft and smooth. Proceed with recipe as directed in Step 3.

ORANGE-PECAN SCONES

Makes: 16 scones   Hands-on Time: 10 min.   Total Time: 22 min.

Orange zest and fresh orange juice give these scones a sweet, tart flavor, while pecans add a subtle crunch.

2   cups self-rising flour
½   cup sugar
2   tsp. orange zest
⅓   cup butter
½   cup buttermilk

¼   cup fresh orange juice
½   cup chopped pecans
1   tsp. vanilla extract
Sugar

1. Preheat oven to 425°. Combine first 3 ingredients. Cut butter into flour mixture with a pastry blender until crumbly; add buttermilk and next 3 ingredients, stirring just until dry ingredients are moistened.

2. Turn dough out onto a lightly floured surface; knead 3 or 4 times.

3. Divide dough in half; pat each portion into a 7-inch circle, and place on a lightly greased baking sheet. Cut each circle into 8 wedges; sprinkle with sugar.

4. Bake at 425° for 12 to 14 minutes or until golden brown.

TO FREEZE IT: Place baked scones in a labeled airtight container up to 1 month. Thaw in fridge 8 hours. Bake scones at 350° for 10 minutes or until thoroughly heated.

SIMPLE SWEET POTATO BISCUITS

Makes: 2 dozen (serving size: 1 biscuit)   Hands-on Time: 15 min.   Total Time: 25 min.

⅓ cup light butter
2¾ cups reduced-fat all-purpose
    baking mix

1   cup mashed sweet potato
½   cup 2% reduced-fat milk

1. Preheat oven to 450°. Cut butter into baking mix with a pastry blender or 2 forks until mixture is crumbly. Whisk together sweet potato and milk; add to butter mixture, stirring with a fork just until dry ingredients are moistened.

2. Turn dough out onto a lightly floured surface; knead gently 4 or 5 times. (Dough will be moist.) Pat or roll dough to ½-inch thickness; cut with a 2-inch round cutter. Place biscuits on lightly greased baking sheets.

TO FREEZE IT: Freeze unbaked biscuits on a lightly greased baking sheet 30 minutes or until frozen. Label and store in a large zip-top plastic freezer bag up to 3 months. Bake as directed in Step 3.

3. Bake at 450° for 10 minutes or until golden brown.

Keep a dozen of these tasty biscuits in the freezer for drop-in company. They're delicious drizzled with a touch of honey.

CHICKEN-ANDOUILLE GUMBO WITH ROASTED POTATOES

Makes: 10 cups   Hands-on Time: 45 min.   Total Time: 3 hr., 10 min.

Warm up and fill up with a big batch of this hearty Southern favorite.

- 1 lb. andouille sausage, cut into ¼-inch-thick slices
- ½ cup peanut oil
- ¾ cup all-purpose flour
- 1 large onion, coarsely chopped
- 1 red bell pepper, coarsely chopped
- 1 cup thinly sliced celery
- 2 garlic cloves, minced
- 2 tsp. Cajun seasoning
- ⅛ tsp. ground red pepper (optional)
- 1 (48-oz.) container chicken broth
- 2 lb. skinned and boned chicken breasts

Roasted Potatoes

Toppings: chopped fresh parsley, cooked and crumbled bacon, hot sauce

1. Cook sausage in a large skillet over medium heat, stirring often, 7 minutes or until browned. Remove sausage; drain and pat dry with paper towels.

2. Heat oil in a Dutch oven over medium heat; gradually whisk in flour, and cook, whisking constantly, 18 to 20 minutes or until caramel-colored. (Do not burn.) Reduce heat to low, and cook, whisking constantly, until milk chocolate-colored and smooth (about 2 minutes).

3. Increase heat to medium. Stir in onion, next 4 ingredients, and, if desired, ground red pepper. Cook, stirring constantly, 3 minutes. Gradually stir in broth; add chicken and sausage. Increase heat to medium-high; bring to a boil. Reduce heat to low; simmer, stirring occasionally, 1 hour and 30 minutes to 1 hour and 40 minutes or until chicken is done. Shred into large pieces using 2 forks. Place Roasted Potatoes in serving bowls. Spoon gumbo over potatoes. Serve immediately with desired toppings.

TO FREEZE IT: Place the pot of soup in a bath of ice water in the sink to cool. Stir often to help release the heat. Ladle into labeled gallon- or quart-size zip-top plastic freezer bags. Let out any excess air, and seal; freeze up to 1 month. To reheat, thaw soup in fridge overnight, and simmer over low heat, stirring occasionally.

roasted potatoes

Makes: about 1½ dozen   Hands-on Time: 10 min.   Total Time: 50 min.

- 3 lb. baby red potatoes, quartered
- 1 Tbsp. peanut oil
- 1 tsp. kosher salt

1. Preheat oven to 450°. Stir together all ingredients in a large bowl. Place potatoes in a single layer in a lightly greased 15- x 10-inch jelly-roll pan. Bake 40 to 45 minutes or until tender and browned, stirring twice.

Most Kentuckians can't imagine Derby Day without this thick meat and vegetable stew. Variations abound, using all kinds of meats such as lamb, veal, and game. Pass hot sauce around the table for those who want a little extra zip.

KENTUCKY BURGOO

Makes: 6 qt.   Hands-on Time: 28 min.   Total Time: 5 hr., 43 min.

1	(3- to 4-lb.) whole chicken	1	cup frozen baby lima beans
1	(2-lb.) beef chuck roast	1	cup frozen English peas
2	lb. pork loin chops, trimmed	3	garlic cloves, minced
1	lb. tomatoes	2	qt. beef broth
5	potatoes	1	(32-oz.) bottle ketchup
5	celery ribs	2	cups dry red wine
4	carrots	1	(10-oz.) bottle Worcestershire sauce
2	onions	¼	cup white vinegar
2	green bell peppers	1	Tbsp. salt
1	small cabbage	1	Tbsp. pepper
2	cups frozen whole kernel corn	1	Tbsp. dried thyme

1. Bring first 3 ingredients and 5 qt. water to a boil in a large heavy stockpot. Cover, reduce heat, and simmer 1 hour or until tender. Remove meats, reserving liquid in stockpot; skin, bone, and shred meats, and return to pot.
2. Chop tomatoes and next 5 ingredients; shred cabbage. Add chopped vegetables, corn, and next 11 ingredients to meats; cook over low heat, stirring often, 4 hours.

TO FREEZE IT: Place the pot of soup in a bath of ice water in the sink to cool. Stir the soup often to help release the heat. Ladle into labeled gallon- or quart-size zip-top plastic freezer bags. Let out any excess air, and seal; freeze up to 1 month. To reheat, thaw soup in fridge overnight, and simmer over low heat, stirring occasionally.

This soup makes a big batch so it's perfect for freezing leftovers. Consider freezing in single-serving containers—handy for lunches or a quick weeknight dinner.

HEARTY ITALIAN SOUP WITH PARMESAN-PEPPER CORNBREAD BISCOTTI

Makes: 12 cups   Hands-on Time: 40 min.   Total Time: 2 hr., 40 min.

1   (16-oz.) package mild Italian sausage
2   tsp. olive oil
1   large onion, diced
2   garlic cloves, minced
1   (48-oz.) container chicken broth
2   (15-oz.) cans cannellini beans, drained and rinsed
2   (14.5-oz.) cans diced tomatoes
1   tsp. dried Italian seasoning
1   (5-oz.) package baby spinach
¼   cup chopped fresh parsley
¼   cup chopped fresh basil
Freshly shredded Parmesan cheese
Parmesan-Pepper Cornbread Biscotti

1. Cook sausage in hot oil in a Dutch oven over medium heat 7 to 8 minutes on each side or until browned. Remove sausage from Dutch oven, reserving drippings in Dutch oven. Sauté onion in hot drippings 3 minutes or until tender. Add garlic, and sauté 1 minute. Cut sausage into ¼-inch-thick slices, and return to Dutch oven.

2. Stir chicken broth and next 3 ingredients into sausage mixture; bring to a boil over medium-high heat. Reduce heat to medium-low, and simmer 25 minutes.

3. Stir in spinach and next 2 ingredients; cook, stirring occasionally, 5 to 6 minutes or until spinach is wilted. Top each serving with Parmesan cheese. Serve with Parmesan-Pepper Cornbread Biscotti.

TO FREEZE IT: Place the pot of soup in a bath of ice water in the sink to cool. Stir the soup often to help release the heat. Ladle into labeled gallon- or quart-size zip-top plastic freezer bags. Let out any excess air, and seal; freeze up to 1 month. To reheat, thaw soup in fridge overnight, and simmer over low heat, stirring occasionally.

parmesan-pepper cornbread biscotti

Makes: about 1½ dozen   Hands-on Time: 15 min.   Total Time: 1 hr., 30 min.

2 (6-oz.) packages buttermilk cornbread-and-muffin mix	¾ tsp. chopped fresh rosemary
1 cup freshly grated Parmesan cheese, divided	¼ cup cold butter, cut into pieces
2 tsp. freshly ground pepper	3 large eggs, divided
	¼ cup buttermilk
	Parchment paper

1. Preheat oven to 350°. Combine cornbread mix, ¾ cup grated Parmesan cheese, and next 2 ingredients in a food processor bowl. Add butter, and pulse 5 or 6 times or until crumbly.

2. Whisk together 2 eggs and buttermilk. With processor running, gradually add egg mixture through food chute, and process just until well moistened. (Batter will be thick.)

3. Spread dough into a 12- x 4-inch rectangle on a parchment paper-lined baking sheet using lightly greased hands. Lightly beat remaining egg; brush over dough. Sprinkle with remaining cheese.

4. Bake at 350° for 20 minutes or until pale golden brown and firm. Let cool on baking sheet on a wire rack 10 minutes. Reduce oven temperature to 300°.

5. Gently slide loaf (on parchment paper) onto a cutting board, and cut loaf diagonally into ½-inch-thick slices using a serrated knife. Place slices, cut sides down, on a baking sheet lined with clean parchment.

6. Bake at 300° for 15 to 20 minutes on each side or until golden and crisp. Cool on baking sheet on wire rack 15 minutes. Serve warm.

TO FREEZE IT: Cool biscotti completely. Store in a labeled, airtight container, and freeze up to 2 weeks.

Jalapeño-Pepper Jack Cornbread Biscotti: Omit pepper and rosemary. Substitute 1 cup (4 oz.) shredded pepper Jack cheese for Parmesan cheese. Add 1 jalapeño pepper, seeded and finely chopped, to food processor in Step 1. Proceed as directed.

Bacon-Cheddar-Chive Cornbread Biscotti: Omit pepper and rosemary. Substitute 1 cup (4 oz.) shredded sharp Cheddar cheese for Parmesan cheese. Add 1 Tbsp. chopped fresh chives and 4 cooked bacon slices, crumbled, to food processor in Step 1. Proceed as directed.

Parmesan-Garlic Cornbread Biscotti: Omit pepper and rosemary. Reduce eggs to 2. Add 1 large garlic clove, minced, and ¼ tsp. salt to food processor in Step 1. Brush 2 Tbsp. melted butter on top of dough rectangle before baking. Proceed as directed.

BEEF VEGETABLE SOUP

Makes: 18 cups   Hands-on Time: 18 min.   Total Time: 1 hr., 13 min.

This beef vegetable soup is the ultimate comfort food to help keep you warm on a chilly winter night.

1½ lb. beef stew meat
1 Tbsp. olive oil
1 (32-oz.) bag frozen mixed vegetables (peas, carrots, green beans, and lima beans)
1 (15-oz.) can tomato sauce
1 (14.5-oz.) can diced Italian-style tomatoes

1 medium baking potato, peeled and diced
1 celery rib, chopped
1 medium onion, chopped
2 garlic cloves, minced
½ cup ketchup
1 extra-large chicken bouillon cube
½ tsp. pepper

1. Cook meat in hot oil over medium-high heat in a large Dutch oven 6 to 8 minutes or until browned.

2. Stir in frozen mixed vegetables, next 9 ingredients, and 1½ qt. water, stirring to loosen particles from bottom of Dutch oven. Bring mixture to a boil over medium-high heat; cover, reduce heat to low, and simmer, stirring occasionally, 55 to 60 minutes or until potatoes are tender.

TO FREEZE IT: Place the pot of soup in a bath of ice water in the sink to cool. Stir the soup often to help release the heat. Ladle into labeled gallon- or quart-size zip-top plastic freezer bags. Let out any excess air, and seal; freeze up to 1 month. To reheat, thaw soup in fridge overnight, and simmer over low heat, stirring occasionally.

flavor profile

An extra-large bouillon cube adds more flavor. If you don't have this size, you can use 2 regular cubes.

Combining all things Southwestern, this classic soup features ground beef, taco seasoning, corn, tomatoes, chiles, and jalapeños. It's the perfect supper solution on chilly weeknights.

SOUTHWESTERN SOUP

Makes: 6 servings   Hands-on Time: 19 min.   Total Time: 55 min.

- 1 lb. ground beef
- 1 cup coarsely chopped onion
- 2 garlic cloves, minced
- 2 (16-oz.) cans light red kidney beans, drained and rinsed
- 1 (15-oz.) can black beans, drained and rinsed
- 1 (14.5-oz.) can petite diced tomatoes and jalapeños, undrained
- 1 (14.5-oz.) can diced tomatoes and mild green chiles, undrained
- 1 (14-oz.) can beef broth
- 2 cups frozen yellow and white whole kernel corn
- 1 (1-oz.) envelope taco seasoning mix
- ¼ tsp. salt
- ¼ tsp. pepper
- 2 Tbsp. chopped fresh cilantro

Toppings: sour cream, chopped fresh cilantro

Blue corn tortilla chips (optional)

1. Brown ground beef, onion, and garlic in a large Dutch oven over medium-high heat, stirring often, 10 to 12 minutes or until meat crumbles and is no longer pink and onion is softened; drain.

2. Stir in kidney beans, next 8 ingredients, and 4 cups water. Bring to a boil over medium-high heat. Cover, reduce heat to low, and simmer 30 minutes or until thoroughly heated. Stir in cilantro just before serving. Serve with desired toppings and tortilla chips, if desired.

TO FREEZE IT: Place the pot of soup in a bath of ice water in the sink to cool. Stir the soup often to help release the heat. Ladle into labeled gallon- or quart-size zip-top plastic freezer bags. Let out any excess air, and seal; freeze up to 1 month. To reheat, thaw soup in fridge overnight, and simmer over low heat, stirring occasionally.

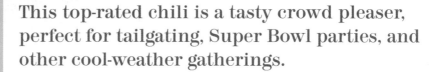

This top-rated chili is a tasty crowd pleaser, perfect for tailgating, Super Bowl parties, and other cool-weather gatherings.

BIG-BATCH CHILI

Makes: 15 to 18 cups   Hands-on Time: 18 min.   Total Time: 4 hr., 18 min.

4   lb. ground chuck
2   medium onions, chopped
1   green bell pepper, chopped
2   garlic cloves, minced
3   (14½-oz.) cans diced tomatoes, undrained
4   (8-oz.) cans tomato sauce
1   (6-oz.) can tomato paste
¼   cup chili powder
1   Tbsp. sugar

1   tsp. salt
1   tsp. pepper
½   tsp. paprika
½   tsp. ground red pepper
1   bay leaf
2   (16-oz.) cans light red kidney beans, drained and rinsed (optional)
Toppings: sour cream, shredded Cheddar cheese, chopped green onions, sliced black olives

1. Brown ground chuck, in batches, in a large Dutch oven. Drain beef, and return to Dutch oven. Add onions, next 12 ingredients, and, if desired, beans. Bring to a boil over medium-high heat; reduce heat, cover, and simmer 4 to 6 hours. Remove and discard bay leaf. Serve with desired toppings.

TO FREEZE IT: Let chili stand 30 minutes. Divide chili mixture into 3 (1-gallon) labeled zip-top plastic freezer bags; seal and lay each bag flat. Stack bags of chili in freezer. Freeze up to 1 month. Thaw frozen chili in fridge overnight, or defrost in microwave. Pour thawed chili into a 9-inch square baking dish. Cover tightly with heavy-duty plastic wrap, and fold back a corner to allow steam to escape. Microwave at HIGH 6 to 7 minutes or until bubbly, stirring after 3½ minutes.

SPICY MEATBALLS

Makes: 10 to 12 servings   Hands-on Time: 30 min.   Total Time: 2 hr.

2   small onions, finely chopped and divided
2   Tbsp. olive oil
1   (10¾-oz.) can tomato purée
¼   cup red wine vinegar
2   to 3 Tbsp. yellow mustard
1   Tbsp. Worcestershire sauce
1   tsp. brown sugar
½   tsp. salt
½   tsp. chili powder

¼   tsp. garlic powder
1   lb. ground beef
1   small jalapeño pepper, seeded and finely chopped
1   large egg, lightly beaten
½   cup cracker meal
½   cup ketchup
1   tsp. salt
1   tsp. pepper
½   tsp. hot sauce

1. Sauté 1 chopped onion in hot oil in a large skillet over medium-high heat 5 minutes or until tender.

2. Add tomato purée, 1 cup water, and next 7 ingredients. Bring to a boil; reduce heat, and simmer, stirring occasionally, 1 hour.

3. Preheat oven to 350°. Combine ground beef, remaining onion, jalapeño pepper, and next 5 ingredients. Shape into 40 (½-inch) balls. Place on a lightly greased rack in a roasting pan.

4. Bake at 350° for 25 minutes or until no longer pink; add to sauce in skillet, stirring gently to coat. Stir in hot sauce just before serving.

TO FREEZE IT: Place cooked or uncooked meatballs in a labeled airtight container, and freeze up to 1 month. Reheat frozen cooked meatballs in a 350° oven 10 to 12 minutes or until thoroughly heated. Bake uncooked frozen meatballs in a 350° oven 25 minutes. Freeze sauce separately; thaw in fridge, and simmer in a saucepan until thoroughly heated.

A host of spices and fresh herbs dresses up this North African–inspired burger.

MOROCCAN HAMBURGERS

Makes: 8 servings   Hands-on Time: 14 min.   Total Time: 2 hr., 30 min.

2   lb. ground beef
1   medium onion, finely chopped
⅓   cup finely chopped fresh parsley
¼   cup fine, dry breadcrumbs
¼   cup finely chopped fresh cilantro
1   large egg
3   garlic cloves, finely chopped
2   tsp. paprika

1   tsp. ground cumin
1   tsp. salt
½   tsp. ground black pepper
¼   tsp. ground red pepper
     Hamburger buns
     Toppings: lettuce, sliced tomatoes,
         sliced red onion

1. Combine first 12 ingredients; gently shape into 8 (4-inch) patties. Cover and chill at least 2 hours.

TO FREEZE IT: Place uncooked hamburger patties in a labeled airtight container, and freeze up to 3 months. Thaw in fridge overnight before grilling.

2. Preheat grill to 350° to 400° (medium-high) heat. Grill, covered with grill lid, 6 to 8 minutes on each side or until beef is no longer pink. Serve on buns with lettuce, sliced tomatoes, and sliced red onion.

COFFEE-CRUSTED BEEF WELLINGTONS

Makes: 8 servings   Hands-on Time: 1 hr., 50 min.   Total Time: 2 hr., 10 min.

Coffee gives classic beef Wellington an intriguing new flavor dimension. For the pastry wrap, we found puff pastry shells easier to work with than sheets. Follow our make-ahead steps that make this fancy entrée easy.

2 tsp. freshly ground coffee	½ cup beef broth
1 tsp. salt	2 Tbsp. butter
¾ tsp. pepper	½ lb. fresh mushrooms, minced
¾ tsp. garlic powder	2 shallots, minced
8 (5- to 6-oz.) center-cut beef tenderloin filets (1½ lb.)	½ tsp. salt
1 Tbsp. olive oil or vegetable oil	½ tsp. pepper
3 Tbsp. butter	½ cup Madeira
¼ cup finely chopped onion	8 frozen puff pastry shells, thawed
¼ cup finely chopped carrot	1 large egg, lightly beaten
¼ cup finely chopped celery	2 large eggs, lightly beaten
2 garlic cloves, minced	2 Tbsp. butter
¾ cup Madeira	2½ Tbsp. all-purpose flour
¾ cup freshly brewed coffee	½ cup whipping cream
	½ tsp. salt

1. Combine first 4 ingredients; stir well. Pat filets dry. Coat both sides of filets with spice rub. Heat oil in a large skillet over medium-high heat until skillet is hot. Sear filets, in 2 batches, 1 to 1½ minutes on each side. Remove filets from skillet; place on a plate, and cover and chill until ready to assemble Wellingtons. (Don't clean skillet.)

2. While filets are chilling, melt 3 Tbsp. butter in same skillet over medium-high heat. Add onion, carrot, celery, and garlic; sauté 5 minutes or until very tender. Add ¾ cup Madeira, brewed coffee, and broth; simmer 5 minutes. Remove from heat.

TO FREEZE IT: Let sauce cool completely. Pour into ice trays, and freeze. Once frozen, place sauce cubes in labeled zip-top plastic freezer bags, and freeze up to 1 month. Thaw cubes in a saucepan over medium heat before using in Step 6.

3. Melt 2 Tbsp. butter in same skillet over medium-high heat. Add mushrooms, shallots, ½ tsp. salt, and ½ tsp. pepper; sauté until liquid evaporates. Add ½ cup Madeira, and cook over medium-high heat until liquid evaporates. Remove from heat; let cool. Cover and chill until ready to assemble Wellingtons.

4. Roll each of 8 puff pastry shells to about ⅛ inch thick on a lightly floured surface; spoon 1 heaping tablespoonful mushroom filling in center of each pastry. Top each with a chilled filet. Brush edges of each pastry square with 1 beaten egg. Wrap 2 opposite sides of pastry over each filet, overlapping them; seal seam with beaten egg. Wrap remaining 2 sides of pastry over filet; seal with beaten egg. Seal any gaps with beaten egg, and press pastry around filet to enclose completely.

TO FREEZE IT: Wrap Wellingtons individually in press-and-seal plastic wrap. Place wrapped Wellingtons in large labeled zip-top plastic freezer bags, and freeze up to 1 month. To prepare beef Wellingtons, do not thaw. Preheat oven to 425°. Bake frozen Wellingtons for 36 minutes as directed in Step 5.

5. To bake, place oven rack on lowest oven shelf; preheat oven to 425°. Place a broiler pan on oven rack; heat pan 5 minutes. Brush tops and sides of frozen Wellingtons with 2 beaten eggs. Carefully place frozen Wellingtons, seam side down, on preheated pan. Bake at 425° for 20 to 25 minutes if unfrozen and 36 minutes if frozen.

6. While Wellingtons bake, melt 2 Tbsp. butter in a saucepan over medium heat; add 2½ Tbsp. flour, and cook, stirring constantly, 1 minute. Add reserved Madeira sauce; cook, stirring constantly, over medium heat 6 to 8 minutes or until slightly thickened. Stir in whipping cream; simmer 5 minutes or until desired thickness. Add ½ tsp. salt. Remove from heat.

7. Arrange baked Wellingtons on a serving platter. Serve with Madeira sauce.

test kitchen tip

We found that preheating a broiler pan for 5 minutes and baking Wellingtons on the lowest oven shelf produced the best baked results with golden, flaky pastry.

PORK PICADILLO EMPANADAS

Makes: 16 empanadas   Hands-on Time: 20 min.   Total Time: 45 min.

- ¾   lb. ground pork
- ½   jalapeño pepper, seeded and minced
- 1   tsp. chili powder
- 1   tsp. ground cumin
- ¾   tsp. ground cinnamon
- ¼   tsp. salt
- ¼   cup golden raisins
- 2   cups chipotle salsa, divided
- 2   Tbsp. fresh lime juice
- 3   Tbsp. chopped almonds, toasted
- 3½ Tbsp. sour cream
- 1   (16.3-oz.) can refrigerated buttermilk biscuits
- 1   large egg, lightly beaten

1. Brown pork in a large nonstick skillet over medium-high heat 8 to 10 minutes or until meat crumbles and is no longer pink; drain. Add jalapeño pepper and next 4 ingredients; cook, stirring occasionally, 2 minutes. Stir in raisins, ½ cup salsa, and lime juice. Remove from heat, and stir in almonds and sour cream. Cool.

2. Separate dough into 8 biscuits. Separate each biscuit in half to make 16 rounds. Roll each round into a 4-inch circle on a lightly floured surface.

3. Spoon pork mixture in center of each dough circle. Fold dough over filling, pressing edges with a fork to seal. Cover with plastic wrap, and chill up to 8 hours.

4. Preheat oven to 350°. Place empanadas on lightly greased baking sheets. Brush with egg.

5. Bake at 350° for 15 to 20 minutes or until golden. Cool 5 minutes on baking sheets. Serve with remaining 1½ cups chipotle salsa.

TO FREEZE IT: Freeze baked empanadas in single layer in labeled gallon-size zip-top plastic freezer bags. To reheat, preheat oven to 350°. Set frozen empanadas on a baking sheet 1 inch apart. Bake empanadas 20 to 25 minutes or until thoroughly heated.

MAKE-AHEAD PORK DUMPLINGS

Makes: 58 dumplings   Hands-on Time: 47 min.   Total Time: 1 hr., 12 min.

Pork, soy sauce, ginger, and a host of other ingredients make up this Chinese favorite. Serve it with chopsticks for a festive appetizer—or it also makes a tasty main dish.

1½ lb. lean boneless pork loin chops, cut into chunks
½ (12-oz.) package 50%-less-fat ground pork sausage
¾ tsp. salt
8 water chestnuts, finely chopped
1 to 2 Tbsp. minced fresh ginger
¼ cup cornstarch
1 tsp. lite soy sauce
¼ cup low-sodium fat-free chicken broth
2 Tbsp. sugar
½ tsp. teriyaki sauce
½ tsp. sesame oil
⅛ cup chopped fresh parsley
2 green onions, diced
1 (16-oz.) package won ton skins
Oyster sauce (optional)
Thai chili sauce (optional)
Ginger dipping sauce (optional)
Soy sauce (optional)

1. Process pork loin in a food processor until finely chopped.

2. Combine pork loin, pork sausage, and next 11 ingredients.

3. Cut corners from won ton skins to form circles. Drop 1 tsp. mixture onto middle of each skin. Gather up skin sides, letting dough pleat naturally. Lightly squeeze the middle while tapping the bottom on a flat surface so it will stand upright.

TO FREEZE IT: Arrange unsteamed dumplings on a baking sheet; freeze for 2 hours. Place in labeled zip-top plastic freezer bags; freeze up to 3 months. To cook dumplings from frozen state, steam for 22 to 25 minutes as directed in Step 4.

4. Arrange dumplings in a bamboo steamer basket over boiling water. Cover and steam 20 to 25 minutes. Serve with sauces, if desired.

ONE-DISH BLACK-EYED PEA CORNBREAD

Makes: 12 appetizer or 6 main-dish servings
Hands-on Time: 13 min.   Total Time: 1 hr., 13 min.

1	lb. hot ground pork sausage
1	medium onion, diced
1	cup white cornmeal
½	cup all-purpose flour
1	tsp. salt
½	tsp. baking soda
2	large eggs, lightly beaten
1	cup buttermilk
½	cup vegetable oil
1	(15-oz.) can black-eyed peas, drained
2	cups (8 oz.) shredded Cheddar cheese
¾	cup cream-style corn
¼	cup chopped pickled jalapeño peppers
1	(4.5-oz.) can chopped green chiles

1. Preheat oven to 350°. Cook sausage and onion in a large skillet over medium-high heat 5 minutes, stirring until sausage crumbles and is no longer pink. Drain.

2. Combine cornmeal, flour, salt, and baking soda. Stir together eggs, buttermilk, and oil until combined. Add to dry ingredients, stirring just until moistened. (Batter will not be smooth.) Add sausage mixture, peas, and remaining ingredients to batter, stirring well.

3. Pour into a greased 13- x 9-inch baking dish.

4. Bake at 350° for 1 hour or until golden and set.

TO FREEZE IT: Freeze baked cornbread up to 1 month. Thaw in fridge overnight. Bake, covered, at 350° for 30 minutes. Uncover and bake 10 more minutes or until thoroughly heated. To reheat directly from the freezer, bake, covered, at 350° for 1 hour. Uncover and bake 10 more minutes or until thoroughly heated.

Uniquely Southern, this recipe works as a hearty appetizer when cut into small squares or as a main dish when paired with a tossed green salad.

test kitchen tip

To lighten, substitute 1 (12-oz.) package reduced-fat sausage, fat-free buttermilk, ½ cup egg substitute, and 2% reduced-fat Cheddar cheese. Reduce oil to 2 Tbsp. Prepare and bake as directed.

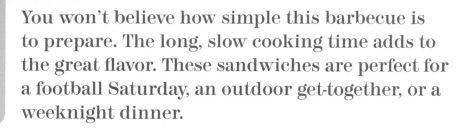

You won't believe how simple this barbecue is to prepare. The long, slow cooking time adds to the great flavor. These sandwiches are perfect for a football Saturday, an outdoor get-together, or a weeknight dinner.

ANYTIME BARBECUE

Makes: 10 servings   Hands-on Time: 20 min.   Total Time: 3 hr., 30 min.

1 (4-lb.) eye of round roast	¼ cup butter
1 tsp. salt	¼ cup lemon juice
3 (8-oz.) cans tomato sauce	2 Tbsp. Worcestershire sauce
1 (12-oz.) bottle chili sauce	½ tsp. dry mustard
1 medium onion, chopped	½ tsp. chili powder
½ cup vinegar	½ tsp. paprika
¼ cup firmly packed brown sugar	Hamburger buns

1. Place roast in large Dutch oven, and sprinkle with salt; add water to cover, and bring to a boil. Cover, reduce heat to medium, and simmer 2 hours or until tender, adding more water as needed after 1 hour.

2. Stir together tomato sauce and next 10 ingredients in a large saucepan; bring to a boil. Reduce heat to low, and simmer 1 hour, stirring occasionally.

3. Remove roast from Dutch oven, and let stand 10 minutes before serving. Shred or slice meat, and serve with hamburger buns and sauce.

Note: We tested with Heinz Chili Sauce.

TO FREEZE IT: Place the meat and sauce in a labeled airtight container, and freeze up to 1 month. To reheat, place in a 13- x 9-inch baking dish. Bake, covered, at 350° for 30 minutes or until bubbly.

CHICKEN CHIMICHANGAS

Makes: 20 servings   Hands-on Time: 55 min.   Total Time: 1 hr., 7 min.

1 (16-oz.) jar picante sauce or salsa, divided	20 (8-inch) flour tortillas
7 cups chopped cooked chicken	3 cups (12 oz.) shredded Cheddar cheese
1 small onion, diced	Vegetable cooking spray
2 to 2½ tsp. ground cumin	Toppings: guacamole, sour cream, shredded lettuce, diced tomato
1½ tsp. dried oregano	
1 tsp. salt	

1. Combine 1½ cups picante sauce and next 5 ingredients in a Dutch oven; cook over medium-low heat, stirring often, 25 minutes or until most of liquid evaporates. Spoon ⅓ cup mixture below center of each tortilla; top with 2 Tbsp. cheese.

2. Preheat oven to 425°. Fold in 2 sides of tortillas to enclose filling. Fold over top and bottom edges of tortillas, making rectangles. Place folded side down on greased baking sheets. Coat chimichangas with cooking spray.

3. Bake at 425° for 12 to 14 minutes. Top with remaining picante sauce and desired toppings.

TO FREEZE IT: Freeze baked chimichangas in a labeled airtight container up to 1 month. To reheat, thaw in fridge overnight. Preheat oven to 425°, and bake for 14 minutes.

Feed a crowd with this Mexican favorite! If the thought of preparing this dish sounds daunting, enlist your group and form an assembly line.

make it a meal

Greet your guests with chips and salsa or cheese dip. Then, serve the main meal with refried beans, Spanish rice, and a salad.

OYSTER DRESSING

Makes: 8 to 10 servings   Hands-on Time: 47 min.   Total Time: 2 hr., 7 min.

Use all 3 cups of broth if you like a really moist dressing.

2 (6-oz.) packages buttermilk cornbread mix
⅓ cup butter
1 cup chopped celery
½ cup chopped onion
1 Tbsp. chopped fresh or 1½ tsp. dried sage
½ tsp. pepper
¼ tsp. salt
4 white bread slices, cut into ½-inch cubes (about 2 cups)
2½ to 3 cups chicken broth
2 large eggs, lightly beaten
1 (12-oz.) container fresh oysters, drained
Garnish: fresh sage leaves

1. Preheat oven to 350°. Prepare cornbread according to package directions for a double recipe. Let cool 30 minutes; crumble into a large bowl.

2. Melt butter in a large skillet over medium heat; add celery and onion, and sauté 10 to 12 minutes or until tender. Stir in sage, pepper, and salt. Stir celery mixture and bread cubes into crumbled cornbread in bowl, stirring gently until blended. Add chicken broth and eggs, and gently stir until moistened; stir in oysters. Spoon mixture into a lightly greased 11- x 7-inch baking dish.

TO FREEZE IT: Prepare recipe as directed through Step 2. Cover with plastic wrap; cover with heavy-duty aluminum foil or container lid. Label and freeze unbaked dressing up to 3 months, if desired. Thaw in fridge overnight. Let stand at room temperature 30 minutes. Bake, uncovered, at 350° for 1 hour and 10 minutes to 1 hour and 15 minutes or until golden.

3. Bake at 350° for 50 to 55 minutes or until golden brown. Garnish, if desired.

Note: We tested with Martha White Cotton Country Cornbread Mix.

This classic recipe makes one large and one small pan of dressing, so freeze one pan for another meal.

CORNBREAD DRESSING

Makes: 16 to 18 servings   Hands-on Time: 52 min.   Total Time: 2 hr., 7 min.

1 cup butter, divided	2 large sweet onions, diced
3 cups self-rising white cornmeal mix	4 celery ribs, diced
1 cup all-purpose flour	¼ cup finely chopped fresh sage
7 large eggs, divided	¼ cup finely chopped fresh parsley
3 cups buttermilk	1 Tbsp. seasoned pepper
3 cups soft, white breadcrumbs	7 cups chicken broth

1. Preheat oven to 425°. Place ½ cup butter in a 13- x 9-inch pan; heat in oven at 425° for 4 minutes. Stir together cornmeal and flour; whisk in 3 eggs and buttermilk.

2. Pour hot butter into batter, and stir until blended. Pour batter into pan.

3. Bake at 425° for 30 minutes or until golden brown. Cool. Crumble cornbread into a large bowl; stir in breadcrumbs, and set aside. Reduce oven temperature to 400°.

4. Melt remaining ½ cup butter in a skillet over medium heat; add onions and celery, and sauté 5 minutes. Stir in sage, parsley, and seasoned pepper; sauté 1 minute. Remove from heat, and stir into cornbread mixture.

5. Whisk together chicken broth and remaining 4 eggs; stir into cornbread mixture. Pour into 1 lightly greased 13- x 9-inch pan and 1 lightly greased 8-inch square pan.

TO FREEZE IT: Prepare recipe as directed through Step 5. Cover with plastic wrap; cover with heavy-duty aluminum foil or container lid. Label and freeze unbaked dressing up to 3 months, if desired. Thaw in fridge overnight. Let stand at room temperature 30 minutes. Bake, uncovered, at 400° for 40 to 45 minutes or until golden.

6. Bake at 400° for 35 to 40 minutes or until golden brown.

CORN-RICE CASSEROLE

Makes: 10 to 12 servings   Hands-on Time: 25 min.   Total Time: 1 hr.

- 2 cups uncooked long-grain rice
- 2 Tbsp. butter
- 1 green bell pepper, chopped
- 1 small onion, chopped
- 1 (14¾-oz.) can cream-style corn
- 1 (11-oz.) can Mexican-style corn, drained
- 1 (11-oz.) can whole kernel corn, drained
- 1 (10-oz.) can diced tomato and green chiles, undrained
- 1 (8-oz.) loaf mild Mexican pasteurized prepared cheese product, cubed
- ½ tsp. salt
- ¼ tsp. pepper
- ½ cup (2 oz.) shredded Cheddar cheese

1. Preheat oven to 350°. Cook rice according to package directions; set aside.

2. Melt butter in a large skillet over medium heat; add bell pepper and onion, and sauté 5 minutes or until tender.

3. Stir in cooked rice, cream-style corn, and next 6 ingredients; cook, stirring occasionally, until cheese melts. Spoon into a lightly greased 13- x 9-inch baking dish.

4. Bake at 350° for 30 minutes or until thoroughly heated; top with shredded cheese, and bake 5 more minutes or until cheese melts.

TO FREEZE IT: Let casserole cool completely. Wrap casserole tightly in aluminum foil, label, and freeze up to 1 month. To reheat, preheat oven to 350°, and bake frozen casserole, covered, for 40 minutes. Uncover and bake 20 more minutes. Let stand 5 minutes.

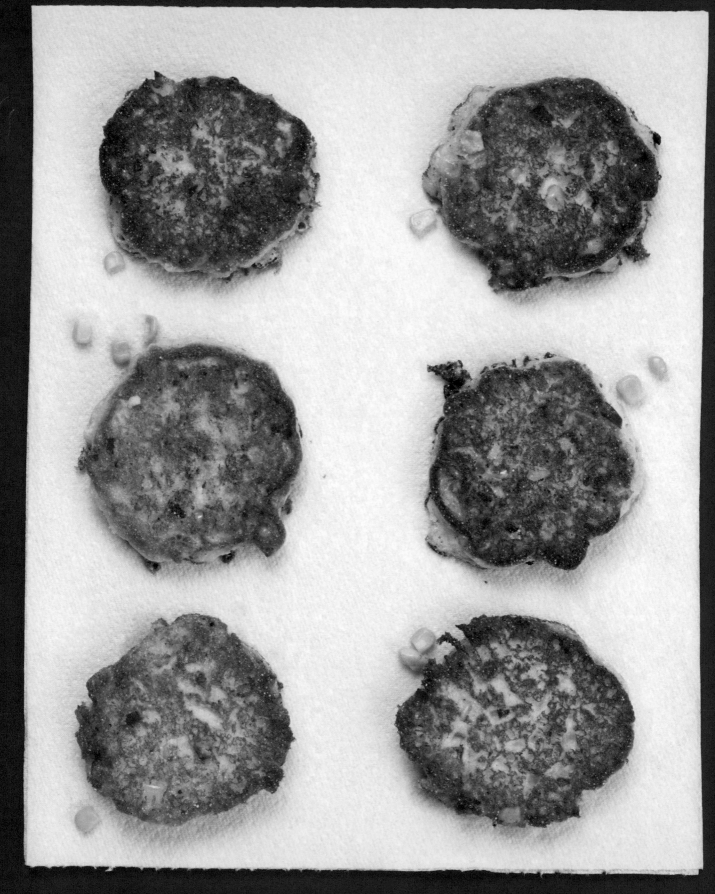

Dress up these cakes with salsa and sour cream and serve as an appetizer. They're also delicious as a side dish, simply smeared with butter.

COUNTRY CORN CAKES

Makes: 14 corn cakes   Hands-on Time: 20 min.   Total Time: 1 hr.

1 (12-oz.) package frozen whole kernel corn, thawed
2 Tbsp. finely chopped onion
2 Tbsp. finely chopped celery
1 (2-oz.) jar diced pimiento, drained

1½ cups buttermilk
1 egg, lightly beaten
2 Tbsp. butter, melted
¼ tsp. salt
1¾ cups self-rising cornmeal mix
¼ cup vegetable oil, divided

1. Finely chop ½ cup corn. Combine chopped and unchopped corn, onion, and next 6 ingredients in a medium bowl; stir well. Gradually add cornmeal, stirring just until moistened.

2. Heat 2 Tbsp. oil in a large skillet over medium-high heat. Pour ¼ cup batter into skillet for each corn cake, cooking 3 or 4 cakes at a time. Cook 4 to 5 minutes on each side or until browned. Drain cakes on paper towels. Repeat procedure using remaining batter and adding oil to skillet, if necessary. Cool.

TO FREEZE IT: Freeze corn cakes in a labeled airtight container up to 1 month. To reheat, place cakes on ungreased baking sheets. Bake at 350° for 10 to 12 minutes or until thoroughly heated.

CROWDER PEA SUCCOTASH

Makes: 8 servings

Hands-on Time: 31 min.   Total Time: 1 hr., 46 min., including crowder peas

½ large onion, finely diced
1 green bell pepper, finely diced
1 red bell pepper, finely diced
3 Tbsp. olive oil
2 cups fresh or frozen corn kernels
Crowder Peas

½ cup reserved Crowder Peas liquid
½ cup sliced green onions
1 Tbsp. fresh thyme leaves, finely chopped
½ tsp. salt

1. Sauté onion and bell peppers in hot oil in a large skillet over medium heat 5 to 7 minutes or until tender. Stir in corn and Crowder Peas; cook 2 minutes or until thoroughly heated. Stir in ½ cup reserved Crowder Peas liquid, green onions, thyme, and salt; cook 1 to 2 minutes or until thoroughly heated. Serve immediately.

TO FREEZE IT: Freeze in labeled zip-top plastic freezer bags up to 1 month. Thaw in fridge overnight. Reheat in a saucepan over medium heat.

crowder peas

Makes: 4 servings   Hands-on Time: 20 min.   Total Time: 55 min.

½ large onion, diced
½ medium carrot, chopped
2 celery ribs, chopped
2 garlic cloves, minced
1 Tbsp. olive oil

2 Tbsp. jarred ham base
2 cups fresh or frozen crowder peas
2 fresh thyme sprigs
½ tsp. salt
½ tsp. pepper

1. Cook first 4 ingredients in hot oil in a Dutch oven over medium-high heat, stirring often, 5 minutes. Stir in ham base and 4 cups of water until well blended. Add peas, thyme, salt, and pepper, and bring mixture to a boil. Reduce heat to low, and simmer 20 minutes or until peas are done. Remove from heat; cool 30 minutes.

2. Drain peas, reserving ½ cup cooking liquid. Remove and discard thyme sprigs.

Note: We tested with Superior Touch Better Than Bouillon ham base.

FREEZER SLAW

Makes: 6 cups   Hands-on Time: 4 min.   Total Time: 10 min.

1½ cups sugar
1   cup cider vinegar
3   (10-oz.) packages shredded
    angel hair cabbage slaw

1   large carrot, shredded
1   small green bell pepper, diced
1   tsp. celery salt
1   tsp. mustard seeds

1. Bring sugar and vinegar to a boil in a small saucepan, stirring until sugar dissolves; cool.

2. Combine cabbage and next 4 ingredients. Pour vinegar mixture over cabbage mixture, tossing to coat.

TO FREEZE IT: Place in a large heavy-duty zip-top plastic freezer bag or airtight container, label, and freeze up to 3 months. Thaw in fridge overnight before serving.

kid
cravings

This crunchy favorite is the perfect topping for yogurt and fruit, and even better on its own as a snack. It makes enough so you can share with friends.

BUTTER-PECAN GRANOLA

Makes: about 8 cups   Hands-on Time: 15 min.   Total Time: 1 hr., 10 min.

½ cup butter, melted
¼ cup honey
2 Tbsp. light brown sugar
1 tsp. vanilla extract
⅛ tsp. salt

3 cups uncooked regular oats
1½ cups coarsely chopped pecans
½ cup wheat germ
2 Tbsp. sesame seeds
1 (10-oz.) package chopped dates

1. Preheat oven to 325°. Stir together butter, honey, brown sugar, vanilla, and salt in a large bowl. Add oats, pecans, wheat germ, and sesame seeds, and stir until mixture is evenly coated.

2. Spread oat mixture on a lightly greased 15- x 10-inch jelly-roll pan. Bake at 325° for 25 to 30 minutes or until toasted, stirring every 10 minutes.

3. Spread granola onto wax paper, and cool completely (about 30 minutes). Stir in chopped dates. Store in an airtight container at room temperature up to 3 days.

TO FREEZE IT: Store granola in a labeled airtight container in freezer up to 6 months. To thaw, remove from freezer, and let stand at room temperature.

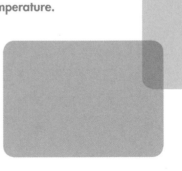

CRANBERRY-PECAN CHEESE WAFERS

Makes: about 18 dozen   Hands-on Time: 30 min.
Total Time: 3 hr., 15 min., plus 8 hr. for chilling

1½ cups chopped pecans
1½ cups coarsely chopped sweetened
     dried cranberries
2   cups butter, softened
4   cups (16 oz.) freshly shredded
     extra-sharp Cheddar cheese

1½ tsp. salt
4   cups all-purpose flour
Parchment paper

1. Preheat oven to 350°. Bake pecans in a single layer in a shallow pan 8 to 10 minutes or until toasted and fragrant, stirring halfway through. Cool completely (about 15 minutes).

2. Meanwhile, soak cranberries in boiling water to cover 15 minutes; drain and pat dry with paper towels.

3. Beat butter and next 2 ingredients at medium speed with a heavy-duty electric stand mixer until blended. Gradually add flour, beating just until combined. Stir in cranberries and pecans. Shape dough into 4 (12-inch-long) logs; wrap each in plastic wrap. Chill 8 hours to 3 days.

4. Preheat oven to 350°. Cut each log into ¼-inch-thick slices; place on parchment paper-lined baking sheets. Bake 13 to 15 minutes or until lightly browned. Remove from baking sheets to wire racks, and cool completely (about 20 minutes).

TO FREEZE IT: Place baked wafers in a labeled airtight container, and freeze up to 3 months.

Tasty and tangy, this refreshing salad is a great way to get kids to eat their fruit.

FROZEN FRUIT SALAD

Makes: 8 servings   Hands-on Time: 7 min.   Total Time: 8 hr., 27 min.

1   (20-oz.) can pineapple chunks in juice, undrained

3   (6-oz.) cans frozen orange juice concentrate, thawed

1½ cups seedless red grapes, cut in half

1½ cups sliced banana

1½ cups grapefruit sections

1. Drain pineapple, reserving juice in a 2-cup liquid measuring cup; add water to measure 1½ cups.

2. Combine pineapple, pineapple liquid, orange juice concentrate, and next 3 ingredients in a large bowl. Pour into a 13- x 9-inch baking dish.

3. Cover with plastic wrap; freeze 8 hours or until firm. Let stand at room temperature 20 minutes; cut into squares.

TO FREEZE IT: Salad can remain labeled and wrapped tightly in the freezer up to 3 weeks.

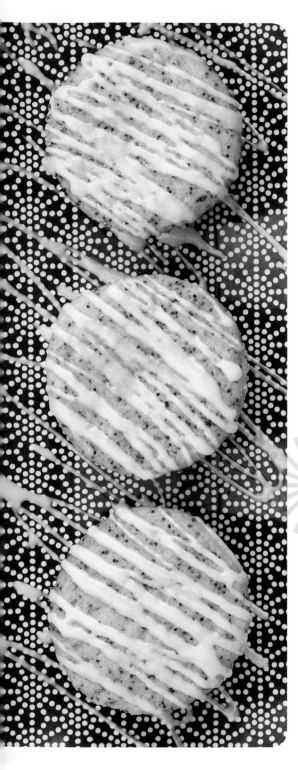

BUTTERMILK-POPPY SEED MUFFINS

Makes: 15 muffins   Hands-on Time: 15 min.
Total Time: 45 min., including glaze

2	cups all-purpose flour	1	cup buttermilk
1	cup sugar	3	large eggs
1	Tbsp. orange zest	2	Tbsp. poppy seeds
1½	tsp. baking powder	1	tsp. vanilla extract
½	tsp. baking soda	½	cup butter, melted
½	tsp. salt		Orange Glaze

1. Preheat oven to 375°. Combine first 6 ingredients in a large bowl; make a well in center of mixture.

2. Whisk together buttermilk and next 3 ingredients in a medium bowl. Add buttermilk mixture to flour mixture, stirring just until dry ingredients are moistened. Stir in melted butter. Spoon batter into lightly greased muffin pans, filling three-fourths full.

3. Bake at 375° for 20 to 25 minutes or until a wooden pick inserted in center comes out clean. Cool in pans on a wire rack 5 minutes. Remove from pans, and cool on wire racks.

TO FREEZE IT: Freeze unglazed muffins in a labeled zip-top plastic freezer bag up to 1 month. To reheat, preheat oven to 350°. Wrap each frozen muffin in foil, and bake at 350° for 25 minutes; remove foil, and bake 5 more minutes. Add glaze after reheating.

4. Drizzle with Orange Glaze.

orange glaze

Makes: about ½ cup   Hands-on Time: 5 min.   Total Time: 5 min.

1	cup powdered sugar	2	Tbsp. orange juice
1	tsp. vanilla extract		

1. Stir together powdered sugar, vanilla, and 1 Tbsp. orange juice. Stir in remaining 1 Tbsp. orange juice, 1 tsp. at a time, for desired consistency.

PEANUT BUTTER-BANANA MUFFINS

Makes: about 1½ dozen   Hands-on Time: 20 min.   Total Time: 1 hr.

2 cups wheat bran cereal shreds

1¾ cups milk

1½ cups all-purpose flour

¾ cup sugar

1 Tbsp. baking powder

¼ tsp. salt

1 medium-size ripe banana, mashed

½ cup chunky peanut butter

¼ cup vegetable oil

1 large egg

Streusel Topping

1. Preheat oven to 350°. Stir together cereal and milk; let stand 5 minutes.

2. Combine flour and next 3 ingredients in a large bowl; make a well in center of mixture.

3. Stir banana and next 3 ingredients into cereal mixture; add to dry ingredients, stirring just until moistened. Spoon into greased muffin pans, filling two-thirds full. Sprinkle Streusel Topping evenly over batter.

4. Bake at 350° for 25 to 30 minutes. Remove from pans immediately, and cool on wire racks.

streusel topping

Makes: 1¼ cups   Hands-on Time: 10 min.   Total Time: 10 min.

½ cup all-purpose flour

½ cup firmly packed light brown sugar

¼ cup butter

2 Tbsp. peanut butter

1. Combine flour and brown sugar. Cut butter and peanut butter into flour mixture with a pastry blender or fork until mixture resembles small peas.

Note: We tested with Kellogg's All-Bran cereal for shreds of wheat bran cereal.

TO FREEZE IT: Place baked muffins in a labeled zip-top plastic freezer bag, and freeze up to 1 month. To serve, remove from freezer, and let thaw at room temperature.

These muffins are great for breakfast or as an afternoon snack. They also make great gifts, so freeze ahead and always have goodies on hand.

APPLESAUCE MUFFINS WITH CINNAMON STREUSEL TOPPING

Makes: 14 muffins   Hands-on Time: 15 min.   Total Time: 48 min., including topping

4 cups all-purpose baking mix	½ cup milk
½ cup sugar	¼ cup vegetable oil
2 tsp. ground cinnamon	2 large eggs
⅔ cup chunky applesauce	Cinnamon Streusel Topping

1. Preheat oven to 400°. Whisk together baking mix, sugar, and cinnamon in a large bowl; make a well in center of mixture.

2. Whisk together applesauce and next 3 ingredients in a small bowl; add to sugar mixture, stirring just until dry ingredients are moistened. Spoon batter into lightly greased muffin pans, filling almost completely full. Sprinkle Cinnamon Streusel Topping over batter.

3. Bake at 400° for 18 to 20 minutes or until a wooden pick inserted in center comes out clean and tops are golden brown. Cool in pans on a wire rack 5 minutes. Remove from pans, and cool on wire racks.

Note: We tested with Bisquick All-Purpose Baking Mix.

cinnamon streusel topping

Makes: about 1 cup   Hands-on Time: 10 min.   Total Time: 10 min.

⅓ cup granulated sugar	3 Tbsp. all-purpose baking mix
¼ cup firmly packed light brown sugar	¼ tsp. ground cinnamon
	2 Tbsp. butter, melted

1. Whisk together first 4 ingredients until blended. Stir melted butter into sugar mixture until well blended and crumbly.

TO FREEZE IT: Place baked muffins in a labeled zip-top plastic freezer bag, and freeze up to 1 month. To serve, remove from freezer, and let thaw at room temperature.

Kids will love working with the crescent roll dough that serves as the base of this tasty anytime treat.

MINI-CINNIS

Makes: 20 rolls   Hands-on Time: 7 min.   Total Time: 17 min.

1 (8-oz.) can refrigerated reduced-fat crescent rolls	Vegetable cooking spray
4 tsp. cinnamon sugar	½ cup powdered sugar
	2 tsp. 1% low-fat milk

1. Preheat oven to 375°. Unroll crescent rolls, and cut dough crosswise with a sharp knife, forming 2 portions. Press perforations together with fingers. Sprinkle each portion of dough with 2 tsp. cinnamon sugar.

2. Roll up 1 portion of dough, starting at long side and pressing firmly to eliminate air pockets; pinch seam to seal. Cut roll into 10 slices. Place slices cut-sides down on a baking sheet coated with cooking spray. Repeat with remaining dough portion.

3. Bake at 375° for 10 to 12 minutes or until rolls are golden.

TO FREEZE IT: Place unglazed cinnamon rolls in a labeled airtight container, and freeze up to 1 month. To reheat, defrost in the microwave, and drizzle with the glaze.

4. Combine powdered sugar and milk in a small bowl, stirring with a whisk until smooth; drizzle over warm rolls with a small whisk.

shortcut secret

To make slicing easier, place unbaked rolls on baking sheet, and freeze for 10 minutes, then slice. This recipe can be easily doubled to serve a crowd.

BACON-AND-CHEDDAR CORN MUFFINS

Makes: 1 dozen   Hands-on Time: 22 min.   Total Time: 52 min.

6 bacon slices
2 cups self-rising white cornmeal mix
1 Tbsp. sugar
1½ cups buttermilk
1 large egg

4 Tbsp. butter, melted
1 cup (4 oz.) shredded sharp Cheddar cheese
Vegetable cooking spray

1. Preheat oven to 425°. Cook bacon in a large skillet over medium-high heat 12 to 14 minutes or until crisp; remove bacon, and drain on paper towels. Crumble bacon.

2. Heat a 12-cup muffin pan in oven 5 minutes.

3. Combine cornmeal mix and sugar in a medium bowl; make a well in center of mixture.

4. Stir together buttermilk and egg; add to cornmeal mixture, stirring just until dry ingredients are moistened. Stir in melted butter, cheese, and bacon. Remove pan from oven, and coat with cooking spray. Spoon batter into hot muffin pan, filling almost completely full.

5. Bake at 425° for 15 to 20 minutes or until golden. Remove from pan, and cool 10 minutes on a wire rack.

Note: We tested with White Lily White Cornmeal Mix.

TO FREEZE IT: Freeze muffins in a labeled zip-top plastic freezer bag up to 1 month. To reheat, preheat oven to 350°. Wrap each frozen muffin in foil, and bake at 350° for 25 minutes; remove foil, and bake 5 more minutes.

Ham-and-Swiss Corn Muffins: Substitute Swiss cheese for Cheddar cheese and 1 cup diced cooked ham for bacon. Reduce butter in batter to 3 Tbsp. Brown ham in remaining 1 Tbsp. melted butter in a nonstick skillet over medium-high heat 5 to 6 minutes. Proceed as directed, whisking in 2 Tbsp. Dijon mustard with buttermilk and egg.

test kitchen tip
Heating the pan beforehand results in a nice crispy muffin bottom.

Serve these scones alongside the Zesty Pizza Sauce on page 20. The pizza sauce can also be made ahead and frozen.

PIZZA SCONES

Makes: 8 scones   Hands-on Time: 15 min.   Total Time: 35 min.

2   cups all-purpose baking mix
¾   cup (3 ounces) shredded sharp Cheddar cheese
¼   cup dried tomatoes, thinly sliced
¼   cup sliced black olives
¼   cup chopped salami
2   Tbsp. cornmeal
½   tsp. onion powder

½   tsp. dried Italian seasoning
3   Tbsp. shredded Parmesan cheese, divided
¾   cup buttermilk
1½ tsp. olive oil
¼   tsp. black pepper
1   cup pizza sauce (optional)

1. Preheat oven to 400°. Combine first 8 ingredients and 2 Tbsp. Parmesan cheese; add buttermilk. Stir until a soft dough forms.

2. Turn dough out onto a lightly floured surface. Pat into an 8-inch circle; place on a lightly greased baking sheet. Brush with oil; sprinkle with pepper and remaining 1 Tbsp. Parmesan cheese. Cut into 8 wedges.

3. Bake at 400° for 15 to 20 minutes or until golden brown. Separate wedges, and serve with pizza sauce, if desired.

TO FREEZE IT: Let the scones cool, and then place in a labeled airtight container, and freeze up to 1 month. To reheat, thaw in the fridge overnight. Preheat oven to 350°, and bake at 350° for 10 minutes or until thoroughly heated.

test kitchen tip

The dough for scones should be rough, and you should try to keep mixing to a minimum for a flaky product.

MORNING GLORY MUFFIN BREAD

Makes: 12 to 16 servings   Hands-on Time: 20 min.   Total Time: 2 hr., 40 min.

1	cup chopped pecans	3	large eggs
3	cups all-purpose flour	2½ tsp.	vanilla extract
1	tsp. salt	1	(8-oz.) can crushed pineapple, undrained
1	tsp. baking soda		
1	tsp. ground cinnamon	2	large carrots, finely grated (1 cup)
½	tsp. ground nutmeg		
2	cups sugar	1	cup golden raisins
¾	cup canola oil		

1. Preheat oven to 350°. Bake pecans in a single layer on a baking sheet 5 to 7 minutes or until lightly toasted and fragrant, stirring halfway through. Cool completely on a wire rack (about 15 minutes).

2. Meanwhile, combine flour and next 4 ingredients in a large bowl; make a well in center of mixture.

3. Whisk together sugar and next 3 ingredients; fold in crushed pineapple and carrots. Add to flour mixture, stirring just until dry ingredients are moistened. Fold in toasted pecans and raisins. Spoon into 2 greased and floured 8- x 4-inch loaf pans.

4. Bake at 350° for 55 to 60 minutes or until a wooden pick inserted in center comes out clean. Cool in pans on a wire racks 15 minutes. Remove from pans to wire racks, and cool completely (about 50 minutes).

TO FREEZE IT: Let bread or muffins cool completely. Place in a labeled zip-top plastic freezer bag, and freeze up to 1 month. To serve, remove from bag, and let thaw at room temperature.

Morning Glory Muffins: Prepare batter as directed. Spoon into lightly greased muffin pans, filling two-thirds full. Preheat oven to 350°. Bake at 350° for 23 to 25 minutes or until a wooden pick inserted in center comes out clean. Cool in pans on wire racks 5 minutes. Remove from pans to wire racks, and cool completely (about 30 minutes). Makes: 2 dozen. Hands-on Time: 30 min. Total Time: 1 hr., 43 min.

CREAM CHEESE-BANANA-NUT BREAD

Makes: 2 loaves   Hands-on Time: 15 min.   Total Time: 2 hr., 10 min.

- 1¼ cups chopped pecans, divided
- ¼ cup butter, softened
- 1 (8-oz.) package ⅓-less-fat cream cheese, softened
- 1 cup sugar
- 2 large eggs
- 1½ cups whole wheat flour
- 1½ cups all-purpose flour
- ½ tsp. baking powder
- ½ tsp. baking soda
- ½ tsp. salt
- 1 cup buttermilk
- 1½ cups mashed very ripe bananas (1¼ lb. unpeeled bananas, about 4 medium)
- ½ tsp. vanilla extract

1. Preheat oven to 350°. Place ¾ cup pecans in a single layer on a baking sheet, and bake 12 to 15 minutes or until toasted and fragrant, stirring after 6 minutes.

2. Beat butter and cream cheese at medium speed with an electric mixer until creamy. Gradually add sugar, beating until light and fluffy. Add eggs, 1 at a time, beating just until blended after each addition.

3. Combine whole wheat flour and next 4 ingredients; gradually add to butter mixture alternately with buttermilk, beginning and ending with flour mixture. Beat at low speed just until blended after each addition. Stir in bananas, ¾ cup toasted pecans, and vanilla. Spoon batter into 2 greased and floured 8- x 4-inch loaf pans. Sprinkle with remaining ½ cup pecans.

4. Bake at 350° for 1 hour or until a long wooden pick inserted in center comes out clean and sides of bread pull away from pan, shielding with aluminum foil during last 15 minutes to prevent excessive browning, if necessary. Cool bread in pans on wire racks 10 minutes. Remove from pans to wire racks. Let cool 30 minutes.

TO FREEZE IT: Cool loaves completely, and wrap tightly with plastic wrap. Wrap again with aluminum foil. Label and freeze up to 1 month. Thaw at room temperature.

Peanut Butter-Cream Cheese-Banana-Nut Bread:
Prepare recipe as directed through Step 3, omitting pecans sprinkled over batter. Combine ¼ cup all-purpose flour and ¼ cup firmly packed brown sugar in a small bowl. Cut in 2 Tbsp. creamy peanut butter and 1½ tsp. butter with a pastry blender or fork until mixture resembles small peas. Lightly sprinkle mixture over batter in pans. Bake and cool as directed.

test kitchen tip

If you've never worked with whole wheat flour, accurate measuring is a must. Be sure to spoon the flour into a dry measuring cup (do not pack), rather than scooping the cup into the flour, and level it off with a straight edge.

Use a light hand when stirring the batter; overmixing will cause a rubbery texture.

PANCAKES WITH BUTTERED HONEY SYRUP

Makes: about 16 (4-inch) pancakes   Hands-on Time: 34 min.   Total Time: 34 min.

1¾ cups all-purpose flour
2 tsp. sugar
1½ tsp. baking powder
1 tsp. baking soda
1 tsp. salt

2 cups buttermilk
2 large eggs
¼ cup butter, melted
Buttered Honey Syrup

1. Combine flour and next 4 ingredients in a large bowl. Whisk together buttermilk and eggs. Gradually stir buttermilk mixture into flour mixture. Gently stir in butter. (Batter will be lumpy.)

2. Pour about ¼ cup batter for each pancake onto a hot buttered griddle or large nonstick skillet. Cook pancakes 3 to 4 minutes or until tops are covered with bubbles and edges look dry and cooked. Turn and cook 3 to 4 minutes or until golden brown. Place pancakes in a single layer on a baking sheet, and keep warm in a 200° oven up to 30 minutes. Serve with warm Buttered Honey Syrup.

TO FREEZE IT: Cool pancakes completely. Wrap individually in plastic wrap. Place in a labeled large zip-top plastic freezer bag, and freeze up to 1 month. To reheat, heat in the microwave on HIGH for 1½ to 2 minutes or until heated through. To reheat in the oven, preheat oven to 300°, and bake at 300° for 10 minutes until heated through.

buttered honey syrup

Makes: about ¾ cup   Hands-on Time: 5 min.   Total Time: 5 min.

⅓ cup butter   ½ cup honey

1. Melt butter in a small saucepan over medium-low heat. Stir in honey, and cook 1 minute or until warm.

Note: Buttered Honey Syrup cannot be made ahead. The heated honey will crystallize when cooled and will not melt if reheated.

ORANGE-GINGER GLAZED CARROTS

Makes: 6 servings   Hands-on Time: 15 min.   Total Time: 45 min.

1   (1-lb.) package crinkle-cut
    carrots
1   tsp. orange zest
¼   cup fresh orange juice
2   tsp. butter

2   tsp. honey
1   to 3 tsp. freshly grated ginger
¼   tsp. salt
⅛   tsp. pepper

1. Stir together all ingredients and 1 cup water in a medium saucepan over medium heat, and bring to a boil. Reduce heat, and simmer, stirring occasionally, 30 to 35 minutes or until liquid is evaporated and carrots are glazed.

TO FREEZE IT: Cool carrots completely. Place in a labeled zip-top plastic freezer bag, and freeze up to 2 months. To serve, thaw in fridge overnight. Reheat in a saucepan over medium heat 5 to 10 minutes or until thoroughly heated.

test kitchen tip

You can substitute 1 tsp. ground ginger for the fresh. Ground ginger is more potent than fresh, so if you opt for the substitution, 1 tsp. will be plenty.

This classic recipe has a soufflé-like texture without the hassle. The result is an impressive side dish the entire family will love.

TEE'S CORN PUDDING

Makes: 8 servings   Hands-on Time: 16 min.   Total Time: 1 hr., 10 min.

12 to 13 ears fresh corn, husks removed	1½ tsp. salt
¼ cup sugar	6 large eggs
3 Tbsp. all-purpose flour	2 cups whipping cream
2 tsp. baking powder	½ cup butter, melted

1. Preheat oven to 350°. Cut kernels from cobs into a large bowl (about 6 cups). Scrape milk and remaining pulp from cobs; discard cobs.

2. Combine sugar and next 3 ingredients. Whisk together eggs, whipping cream, and butter in a large bowl. Gradually add sugar mixture to egg mixture, whisking until smooth; stir in corn. Pour mixture into a lightly greased 13- x 9-inch baking dish.

3. Bake at 350° for 40 to 45 minutes or until set. Let stand 5 minutes.

TO FREEZE IT: Let casserole cool completely. Wrap casserole tightly with aluminum foil, label, and freeze up to 1 month. To reheat, preheat oven to 350°, and bake frozen casserole, covered, for 40 minutes. Uncover and bake 20 more minutes. Let stand 5 minutes.

Stuffed with cheese, bacon, butter, and green onions, twice-baked potatoes are a favorite comfort food and can be served as either a main dish or side.

CHEDDAR-BACON TWICE-BAKED POTATOES

Makes: 6 servings   Hands-on Time: 16 min.   Total Time: 1 hr., 16 min.

- 6 medium-size baking potatoes
- 2 Tbsp. vegetable oil
- 1½ tsp. kosher salt
- ½ cup cream cheese, softened
- ¼ cup butter, softened
- ⅓ cup milk
- 1 cup (4 oz.) shredded sharp Cheddar cheese
- 6 fully cooked bacon slices, crumbled
- 2 green onions, chopped
- ½ tsp. salt
- ½ tsp. pepper

1. Preheat oven to 425°. Prick potatoes several times with a fork; place in a large zip-top bag. Add oil and kosher salt; seal and turn bag to coat. Remove potatoes from bag, and place on a baking sheet. Bake at 425° for 1 hour or until tender. Remove from oven, and cool.

2. Cut a 3-inch-wide strip from top of each potato; discard strips. Scoop pulp into a large bowl, leaving shells intact. Add cream cheese, butter, and milk to pulp in bowl; mash with a potato masher. Stir in cheese and remaining ingredients. Spoon into shells.

TO FREEZE IT: Wrap each potato in aluminum foil; freeze in a labeled large zip-top plastic freezer bag up to 1 month. To reheat, remove desired number of potatoes from bag; unwrap and discard foil. Preheat oven to 350°, and bake for 1 hour or until thoroughly heated.

3. Preheat oven to 350°. Bake thawed potatoes at 350° for 30 minutes.

shortcut secret

To prepare the potato even faster, microwave it instead of baking it. Microwave 1 potato at MEDIUM-HIGH (70% power) for 6 minutes, or microwave 2 potatoes at MEDIUM-HIGH for 8 minutes or until hot.

Yukon gold potatoes yield a texture that's just right for holding a pool of flavorful gravy or melted butter.

PERFECT MASHED POTATOES

Makes: about 6 cups   Hands-on Time: 10 min.   Total Time: 42 min.

3 lb. Yukon gold potatoes
2 tsp. salt, divided
⅓ cup butter

⅓ cup half-and-half
4 oz. cream cheese, softened
¾ tsp. coarsely ground pepper

1. Peel potatoes, and cut into 1-inch pieces. Bring potatoes, 1 tsp. salt, and cold water to cover to a boil in a medium-size Dutch oven over medium-high heat. Reduce heat to medium-low, and cook 16 to 20 minutes or until fork-tender; drain.

2. Return potatoes to Dutch oven. Cook until water evaporates and potatoes look dry. Mound potatoes on 1 side; add butter, next 3 ingredients, and remaining 1 tsp. salt to opposite side of Dutch oven. Cook 1 to 2 minutes or until butter is melted and mixture boils.

3. Remove from heat; beat at medium speed with a handheld mixer 30 seconds to 1 minute or to desired degree of smoothness. (Do not overbeat.)

TO FREEZE IT: Spoon mashed potatoes into an 8-inch square baking dish. Cover tightly with foil, and freeze up to 1 month. To reheat, preheat oven to 350°, and bake frozen casserole, covered, at 350° for 1 hour and 15 minutes or until bubbly.

CORNFLAKE, PECAN, AND MARSHMALLOW-TOPPED SWEET POTATO CASSEROLE

Makes: 8 servings   Hands-on Time: 20 min.   Total Time: 2 hr., 30 min.

Win raves with this seasonal favorite. A crunchy topping balances the creamy smooth, bright orange sweet potatoes.

Sweet Potato Filling:
2½ lb. sweet potatoes (about 5 medium)
2   Tbsp. butter, softened
½   cup firmly packed brown sugar
½   cup 2% reduced-fat milk
1   large egg
½   tsp. salt
½   tsp. vanilla extract

Vegetable cooking spray
Topping:
1¼ cups cornflakes cereal, crushed
¼   cup chopped pecans
1   Tbsp. brown sugar
1   Tbsp. melted butter
1¼ cups miniature marshmallows

1. Prepare filling: Preheat oven to 400°. Bake sweet potatoes on a baking sheet 1 hour or until tender. Reduce oven temperature to 350°. Let potatoes stand until cool to touch (about 20 minutes); peel and mash with a potato masher.

2. Beat mashed sweet potatoes, 2 Tbsp. softened butter, and next 5 ingredients at medium speed with an electric mixer until smooth. Spoon mixture into an 11- x 7-inch baking dish coated with cooking spray.

TO FREEZE IT: Prepare casserole through Step 2. Wrap casserole tightly with foil, label, and freeze up to 1 month. To reheat, thaw in fridge overnight. Proceed with directions in Step 3.

3. Prepare topping: Stir together crushed cornflakes cereal and next 3 ingredients. Sprinkle over sweet potato mixture.

4. Bake at 350° for 30 minutes. Remove from oven; let stand 10 minutes.

Pecan-Topped Sweet Potato Casserole: Omit Cornflake, Pecan, and Marshmallow Topping. Pulse 3 Tbsp. all-purpose flour and ¼ cup firmly packed brown sugar in a food processor until combined. Add 1 Tbsp. cold butter, cut into small pieces, and process 45 seconds or until mixture is crumbly; stir in ⅓ cup finely chopped pecans. Sprinkle mixture over Sweet Potato Filling in baking dish. Bake at 350° for 40 to 45 minutes or until topping is golden brown. Hands-on Time: 20 min.; Total Time: 2 hr., 20 min.

CHEESY CHILI HASH BROWN BAKE

Makes: 8 servings   Hands-on Time: 12 min.   Total Time: 57 min.

1½ lb. lean ground beef or turkey
1 (15.5-oz.) can original sloppy joe sauce
1 (15-oz.) can chili with beans
½ (30-oz.) package frozen country-style shredded hash browns (about 4 cups)

2 cups (8 oz.) shredded Cheddar cheese
Garnish: chopped fresh parsley

1. Preheat oven to 425°. Brown ground beef in a large skillet over medium-high heat, stirring often, 7 to 10 minutes or until meat crumbles and is no longer pink. Stir in sloppy joe sauce and chili.

2. Spoon chili mixture into 8 lightly greased 10-oz. ramekins (or to freeze, place in a lightly greased 13- x 9-inch baking dish, see below). Top with frozen hash browns.

TO FREEZE IT: Place mixture in a lightly greased 13- x 9-inch baking dish, covered tightly in foil, and place in a labeled large zip-top plastic freezer bag, and freeze up to 1 month. Thaw in fridge overnight. Preheat oven to 350°. Bake, covered, for 45 minutes or until heated through. Uncover and bake 10 more minutes. Top with cheese, and bake until cheese is melted.

3. Bake, covered, at 425° for 30 minutes; uncover and bake 10 more minutes or until browned and crisp. Sprinkle with cheese, and bake 5 more minutes or until cheese is melted. Garnish, if desired.

Note: We tested with Manwich Original Sloppy Joe Sauce and Hormel Chili with Beans. Chili mixture can be baked in a lightly greased 13- x 9-inch baking dish as directed.

make it a meal

For an easy side, cook 1 (10-oz.) package frozen broccoli spears in butter sauce according to package directions. Sprinkle with ½ tsp. lemon pepper.

BEEF LOMBARDI

Makes: 6 servings   Hands-on Time: 51 min.   Total Time: 1 hr., 31 min.

1 lb. lean ground beef
1 (14½-oz.) can chopped tomatoes
1 (10-oz.) can diced tomatoes and
   green chiles
2 tsp. sugar
2 tsp. salt
¼ tsp. pepper
1 (6-oz.) can tomato paste
1 bay leaf
1 (6-oz.) package medium
   egg noodles

6 green onions, chopped
   (about ½ cup)
1 cup sour cream
1 cup (4 oz.) shredded
   sharp Cheddar cheese
1 cup shredded Parmesan cheese
1 cup (4 oz.) shredded
   mozzarella cheese
Garnish: sliced green onions

1. Preheat oven to 350°. Brown ground beef in a large skillet over medium heat 5 to 6 minutes, stirring until it crumbles and is no longer pink; drain.

2. Stir in chopped tomatoes and next 4 ingredients; cook 5 minutes. Add tomato paste and bay leaf, and simmer 30 minutes.

3. Cook egg noodles according to package directions; drain.

4. Stir together cooked egg noodles, chopped green onions, and sour cream until blended.

5. Place noodle mixture in bottom of a lightly greased 13- x 9-inch baking dish. Top with beef mixture; sprinkle with cheeses.

TO FREEZE IT: Wrap casserole tightly with aluminum foil, and freeze up to 1 month. To reheat, thaw in fridge overnight. Bake as directed in Step 6.

6. Bake, covered with aluminum foil, at 350° for 35 minutes. Uncover casserole, and bake 5 more minutes. Garnish, if desired.

make it a meal

Serve this casserole with mixed salad greens and garlic bread for a tasty weeknight supper.

CHEESE-AND-TAMALE PIE

Makes: 8 servings   Hands-on Time: 30 min.   Total Time: 50 min.

1   lb. ground chuck
1   large onion, chopped
1   large green bell pepper, chopped
½   cup salsa
1   (15.5-oz.) can pinto beans, drained
1   (14.5-oz.) can diced chili-style or
      regular tomatoes, drained

½   tsp. salt
½   cup chopped fresh cilantro
2   cups (8 oz.) shredded sharp
      Cheddar cheese, divided
1⅓ cups self-rising yellow cornmeal mix
1   cup milk
1   large egg, lightly beaten

1. Preheat oven to 400°. Brown first 3 ingredients in a large skillet, stirring until beef crumbles and is no longer pink. Drain and pat dry with paper towels. Return meat mixture to pan; stir in salsa, beans, tomatoes and salt. Simmer 5 minutes. Stir in cilantro. Spoon mixture into a greased 11- x 7-inch baking dish. Sprinkle with 1 cup cheese.

2. Whisk together cornmeal, milk, and egg in a medium bowl. Stir in remaining 1 cup cheese. Spread batter over beef mixture. Bake at 400° for 20 minutes or until cornbread is lightly browned.

TO FREEZE IT: Cool casserole completely. Cover tightly with aluminum foil; label and freeze up to 3 months. Preheat oven to 350°. Remove casserole from the freezer, and bake at 350° for 1 hour or until thoroughly heated.

ITALIAN STEAK

Makes: 4 to 6 servings   Hands-on Time: 21 min.   Total Time: 2 hr., 21 min.

1   (2-lb.) flank steak   Italian Marinade (page 19)

1. Place flank steak and Italian Marinade in a large zip-top plastic freezer bag. Seal; chill 2 hours.

TO FREEZE IT: Freeze marinated flank steak in a labeled large zip-top plastic freezer bag up to 6 months. To prepare, thaw in the fridge overnight. Grill as directed.

2. Preheat grill to 350° to 400° (medium-high) heat. Grill, covered with grill lid, 8 minutes on each side or to desired degree of doneness. Cut into thin slices, and serve immediately.

MEDITERRANEAN STEAK

Makes: 4 to 6 servings   Hands-on Time: 26 min.   Total Time: 26 min.

Mediterranean Rub (page 18)   1   (2-pound) flank steak
1 Tbsp. olive oil

1. Stir together Mediterranean Rub and olive oil; rub over steak.

TO FREEZE IT: Freeze marinated flank steak in a labeled large zip-top plastic freezer bag up to 6 months. To prepare, thaw in the fridge overnight. Grill as directed.

2. Preheat grill to 350° to 400° (medium-high) heat. Grill, covered with grill lid, 8 minutes on each side or to desired degree of doneness. Cut into thin slices, and serve immediately.

PENNE CASSEROLE

Makes: 8 servings   Hands-on Time: 30 min.   Total Time: 45 min.

1   lb. uncooked penne pasta
½   lb. ground Italian sausage
½   lb. ground beef
½   medium onion, chopped
1   (28-oz.) can whole tomatoes, chopped
1   (6-oz.) can tomato paste
1   garlic clove, minced
1   Tbsp. olive oil
1   Tbsp. red wine

1   tsp. dried basil
1   tsp. dried oregano
¼   tsp. dried crushed red pepper
½   tsp. salt
¼   tsp. pepper
2   cups fresh spinach
2   cups (8 oz.) shredded mozzarella cheese
½   cup shredded Parmesan cheese

1. Preheat oven to 375°. Cook pasta according to package directions; drain and set aside.

2. Brown sausage and ground beef in a large skillet over medium-high heat, stirring often, 7 to 10 minutes or until meat crumbles and is no longer pink. Drain and pat dry with paper towels; keep warm.

3. Add onion and next 10 ingredients to skillet. Simmer over low heat 10 minutes. Stir in meat and spinach; cook just until spinach wilts. Stir in reserved pasta until well combined. Spoon into a lightly greased 13- x 9-inch baking dish. Sprinkle with cheeses.

TO FREEZE IT: Wrap casserole tightly in aluminum foil, and freeze up to 1 month. To reheat, thaw in fridge overnight. Bake as directed in Step 4.

4. Bake, uncovered, at 375° for 15 minutes or until cheese is golden and bubbly.

This casserole would be perfect during the busy holiday season to make ahead for Christmas morning. Or, prepare it to serve breakfast for dinner.

SAUSAGE-AND-EGG CASSEROLE

Makes: 10 servings   Hands-on Time: 20 min.   Total Time: 45 min.

8   (1½-oz.) sourdough bread slices,
    cut into ½-inch cubes
1   (12-oz.) package fully cooked pork
    sausage patties, chopped
2½ cups 2% reduced-fat milk
4   large eggs

1   Tbsp. Dijon mustard
½   cup buttermilk
1   (10¾-oz.) can cream of
    mushroom soup
1   cup (4 oz.) shredded sharp
    Cheddar cheese

1. Preheat oven to 350°. Arrange bread in 2 greased 8-inch square baking dishes or 1 greased 13- x 9-inch baking dish. Proceed as directed, increasing bake time to 1 hour or until casserole is set. Top with sausage. Whisk together milk, eggs, and Dijon mustard. Pour over bread mixture.

2. Whisk together buttermilk and cream of mushroom soup. Spoon over bread mixture; sprinkle with Cheddar cheese.

TO FREEZE IT: Wrap unbaked casserole with plastic wrap, then foil, and label and freeze up to 1 month. To reheat, thaw in the fridge overnight. Bake as directed in Step 3.

3. Bake at 350° for 25 to 30 minutes or until casserole is set and puffed. Serve immediately.

We prefer turkey pepperoni, so you don't get a greasy appearance.

PIZZA SPAGHETTI CASSEROLE

Makes: 6 servings   Hands-on Time: 30 min.   Total Time: 1 hr., 10 min.

12 oz. uncooked spaghetti
½ tsp. salt
1 (1-lb.) package mild ground pork sausage
2 oz. turkey pepperoni slices (about 30), cut in half

1 (26-oz.) jar tomato-and-basil pasta sauce
¼ cup grated Parmesan cheese
1 (8-oz.) package shredded Italian three-cheese blend

1. Preheat oven to 350°. Cook spaghetti with salt according to package directions. Drain well, and place in a lightly greased 13- x 9-inch baking dish.

2. Brown sausage in a large skillet over medium-high heat, stirring occasionally, 5 minutes or until meat crumbles and is no longer pink. Drain and set aside. Wipe skillet clean. Add pepperoni, and cook over medium-high heat, stirring occasionally, 4 minutes or until slightly crisp.

3. Top spaghetti in baking dish with sausage; pour pasta sauce over sausage. Arrange half of pepperoni slices over pasta sauce. Sprinkle with cheeses. Arrange remaining half of pepperoni slices over cheese.

TO FREEZE IT: Wrap unbaked casserole with plastic wrap, then foil, and label and freeze up to 1 month. To reheat, thaw in the fridge overnight; let stand 30 minutes at room temperature, and bake as directed.

4. Cover casserole with nonstick or lightly greased aluminum foil. Bake at 350° for 30 minutes; remove foil, and bake 10 more minutes or until cheese is melted and just begins to brown.

Pepperoni pizza is a classic favorite, and in less than 20 minutes, you can make this tasty version.

PEPPERONI PIZZA

Makes: 6 servings   Hands-on Time: 5 min.   Total Time: 25 min.

3   (8-oz.) portions of Pizza Dough (page 28)

3   cups Zesty Pizza Sauce (page 20)

¼   cup turkey pepperoni slices (about 24)

1½ cups (6 oz.) part-skim mozzarella cheese

1. Preheat oven to 450°. Roll Pizza Dough into 3 (12-inch) circles. Place on greased baking sheets.

2. Spread 1 cup pizza sauce on each pizza crust, leaving a 1-inch border around edges. Top each with pepperoni slices. Sprinkle with cheese.

TO FREEZE IT: Cover pizzas tightly with plastic wrap, and wrap with aluminum foil; label and freeze up to 1 month. To prepare, remove from freezer, and thaw in fridge overnight. Bake as directed in Step 3.

3. Bake pizza at 450° for 20 minutes or until golden.

Simmering the meatballs in the Marinara Sauce is the secret to keeping this delicious Italian dish juicy and tender.

ITALIAN MEATBALLS

Makes: 30 meatballs (6 to 8 servings)   Hands-on Time: 20 min.   Total Time: 55 min.

½ lb. mild Italian sausage, casings removed
¾ lb. ground turkey
1 cup fine, dry breadcrumbs
¾ cup minced onion
4 large eggs, lightly beaten
¾ cup grated Parmesan cheese
1 Tbsp. minced garlic

½ tsp. salt
½ tsp. pepper
2 tsp. dried Italian seasoning
6 cups Marinara Sauce (page 21)
Hot cooked spaghetti
Freshly grated Parmesan cheese (optional)

1. Combine sausage, ground turkey, and next 8 ingredients in a large bowl until well blended.

2. Gently shape meat mixture into 30 (1½-inch) balls.

TO FREEZE IT: Preheat oven to 350°. Bake meatballs at 350° for 20 minutes or until a meat thermometer registers 165° and meatballs are no longer pink in the middle. Let meatballs cool. Freeze meatballs on a baking sheet lined with wax paper for 1 hour. Once frozen, place in a labeled large zip-top plastic freezer bag up to 1 month. To reheat, instead of following Steps 3 and 4, bring sauce to boil in Dutch oven over medium heat. Add frozen meatballs, reduce heat, and simmer, uncovered, 15 minutes or until thoroughly heated.

3. Bring Marinara Sauce to a boil in a Dutch oven over medium heat, stirring occasionally; reduce heat, and simmer. Add 10 meatballs, and cook 6 to 8 minutes or until meatballs are done. Remove meatballs from sauce, and keep warm; repeat procedure with remaining meatballs.

4. Return all cooked meatballs to sauce, reduce heat to low, and cook 10 more minutes.

5. Serve over hot cooked spaghetti, and, if desired, sprinkle with Parmesan cheese.

Take a break from pork and try chicken. Simply serve on buns with extra sauce and pickles. Round out your meal with chips or slaw.

SLOW-COOKED BARBECUED CHICKEN

Makes: 6 servings   Hands-on Time: 20 min.   Total Time: 5 hr., 20 min.

2   tsp. salt
1½ tsp. paprika
½   tsp. garlic powder
½   tsp. pepper
1   (3- to 3½-lb.) cut-up whole chicken

⅔   cup cola soft drink
⅓   cup ketchup
¼   cup firmly packed light brown sugar
2   Tbsp. apple cider vinegar
1   lemon, sliced

1. Stir together first 4 ingredients in a small bowl. Sprinkle over chicken. Place chicken in a single layer in a lightly greased 6-qt. slow cooker.

2. Whisk together cola soft drink and next 3 ingredients in a small bowl. Slowly pour mixture between chicken pieces (to avoid removing spices from chicken). Place lemon slices in a single layer on top of chicken.

3. Cover and cook on HIGH 5 hours (or on LOW 6½ to 7½ hours) or until done.

4. Transfer chicken pieces to a serving platter; discard lemon slices. Skim fat from pan juices in slow cooker. Pour pan juices over chicken; serve immediately.

TO FREEZE IT: Cool chicken completely. Freeze in a labeled airtight container up to 3 months. To serve, thaw in the fridge overnight.

test kitchen tip
Budget-friendly skin-on, bone-in chicken thighs may be substituted (about 2½ lb.).

Get your kids to roll up their sleeves and take part in preparing this meal. They're sure to love it!

CRUNCHY RANCH TORTILLA CHICKEN

Makes: 6 servings   Hands-on Time: 10 min.   Total Time: 23 min.

1   (1-oz.) envelope Ranch-style
     dressing mix, divided
2   lb. chicken breast tenders
¼   cup buttermilk
1   large egg

½   cup all-purpose flour
1   (13-oz.) package Ranch-flavored
     tortilla chips, finely crushed
Vegetable cooking spray

1. Preheat oven to 450°. Sprinkle 1 Tbsp. dressing mix over chicken.

2. Whisk together buttermilk, egg, and remaining dressing mix. Place flour and crushed tortilla chips in separate shallow dishes. Dredge chicken tenders in flour; dip in buttermilk mixture, and roll in crushed chips. Coat chicken lightly on all sides with cooking spray. Set aside.

3. Place a large baking sheet in oven for 5 minutes. Place chicken on hot pan. Bake at 450° for 18 minutes or until crust is lightly browned.

TO FREEZE IT: Cool chicken completely. Place in a labeled large zip-top plastic freezer bag, and freeze up to 1 month. To reheat, preheat oven to 425°. Remove desired amount of chicken from freezer bag, and place on a baking sheet. Bake at 425° for 20 minutes or until hot and crisp.

Double the recipe and serve this to a crowd of kids at your next gathering.

OVEN-FRIED PARMESAN CHICKEN STRIPS

Makes: 5 servings   Hands-on Time: 15 min.   Total Time: 45 min.

2 Tbsp. butter	1½ tsp. Old Bay seasoning
⅓ cup reduced-fat baking mix	⅛ tsp. pepper
⅓ cup grated Parmesan cheese	2 lb. chicken breast strips

1. Preheat oven to 425°. Melt butter in a 15- x 10-inch jelly-roll pan in oven.

2. Place baking mix and next 3 ingredients in a large zip-top plastic freezer bag; shake well to combine. Add chicken, several pieces at a time, shaking well to coat. Arrange chicken in melted butter in hot baking dish.

TO FREEZE IT: Place uncooked, coated chicken strips on a baking sheet in the freezer. Once frozen, place strips in a labeled zip-top plastic freezer bag, and freeze up to 1 month. To reheat, preheat oven to 425°. Bake frozen strips on a hot buttered jelly-roll pan at 425° for 35 minutes, turning after 25 minutes.

3. Bake at 425° for 30 minutes or until chicken is done, turning once. Serve immediately.

Note: We tested with Bisquick Heart Smart Baking Mix.

make it a meal

Ranch dressing, honey mustard, and ketchup all make great dippers. Serve with cut veggies such as celery and carrots.

Green chiles rev up this Southwest-inspired dish that doubles as an appetizer or a side. Serve it as an appetizer with the avocado cream, as well as sour cream and salsa. It makes about 10 appetizer servings.

SOUTHWESTERN CHICKEN-AND-CORN CAKES WITH AVOCADO CREAM

Makes: 5 servings   Hands-on Time: 28 min.   Total Time: 1 hr., 38 min.

1 (12-ounce) package frozen corn soufflé
3 cups finely chopped cooked chicken
1 (4.5-oz.) can chopped green chiles
1 (7-oz.) jar roasted red bell peppers, drained and chopped
7 green onions, chopped
1½ tsp. chili powder
⅛ tsp. salt

⅛ tsp. pepper
2 cups fine, dry breadcrumbs, divided
¾ cup sour cream
1 (6-oz.) package frozen avocado dip, thawed
¼ cup vegetable oil
Garnish: fresh cilantro sprigs

1. Thaw corn soufflé in microwave at MEDIUM (50% power) 6 to 7 minutes.

2. Combine corn soufflé and next 7 ingredients in a large bowl; stir in ½ cup breadcrumbs. Cover and chill 1 hour or overnight.

3. Combine sour cream and avocado dip; set mixture aside.

4. Shape corn mixture into 10 patties, and coat with remaining 1½ cups breadcrumbs.

5. Cook half of corn cakes in 2 Tbsp. hot oil in a large skillet over medium-high heat 3 to 4 minutes on each side or until cakes are golden brown. Drain on paper towels. Repeat procedure with remaining oil and cakes. Serve with avocado cream. Garnish, if desired.

TO FREEZE IT: Let corn cakes cool completely. Place in a labeled zip-top plastic freezer bag, and freeze up to 1 month. To reheat, preheat oven to 350°. Place corn cakes on a baking sheet. Bake at 350° for 25 to 30 minutes.

ZESTY CHICKEN KABOBS

Makes: 6 servings   Hands-on Time: 36 min.   Total Time: 8 hr., 36 min.

2 lb. boned and skinned chicken
   breasts, cut into 1-inch cubes
Zesty Chicken Marinade (page 18)
4 ears corn on the cob, cut into
   1½-inch pieces

2 pt. cherry tomatoes
Garnish: chopped fresh cilantro

1. Place chicken pieces and marinade in a large zip-top plastic freezer bag. Seal; chill 8 hours.

TO FREEZE IT: Freeze marinated chicken in a labeled zip-top plastic freezer bag up to 6 months. To prepare, thaw in the fridge overnight. Grill as directed.

2. Preheat grill to 350° to 400° (medium-high) heat. Soak 8 (8-inch) wooden skewers in water 30 minutes. Remove chicken from marinade, discarding marinade. Thread chicken, corn, and tomatoes onto skewers.

3. Grill, covered with grill lid, 6 to 8 minutes on each side or until done. Garnish, if desired.

make it a meal

For an easy side, toss 1 (5-oz.) head Bibb lettuce with ½ cup drained mandarin oranges. Serve with bottled ginger dressing.

Kids and adults alike will love the delectable taste of this sweet treat. Serve the ice cream in waffle bowls with sprinkles for an added bit of fun.

COCONUT PIE ICE CREAM

Makes: about 1 qt.   Hands-on Time: 5 min.   Total Time: 9 hr., 17 min.

¾ cup sugar
2 Tbsp. cornstarch
⅛ tsp. salt
1 cup milk
1 cup coconut milk
1 cup heavy whipping cream

1 egg yolk
1½ tsp. vanilla extract
¾ cup sweetened flaked coconut, toasted
Garnish: assorted sprinkles

1. Whisk together first 3 ingredients in a large heavy saucepan. Gradually whisk in milk, coconut milk, and cream. Cook over medium heat, stirring constantly, 10 to 12 minutes or until mixture thickens slightly. Remove from heat.

2. Whisk egg yolk until slightly thickened. Gradually whisk about 1 cup hot cream mixture into yolk. Add yolk mixture to remaining hot cream mixture, whisking constantly. Whisk in vanilla. Cool 1 hour, stirring occasionally.

3. Place plastic wrap directly on cream mixture, and chill 8 to 24 hours.

4. Stir in toasted coconut. Pour mixture into freezer container of a 1½-qt. electric ice-cream maker, and freeze according to manufacturer's instructions. Garnish, if desired.

TO FREEZE IT: Place ice cream in a labeled airtight container, and store in the freezer up to 1 month.

STRAWBERRY-ORANGE POPS

Makes: 12 pops   Hands-on Time: 10 min.   Total Time: 8 hr., 10 min.

2   cups orange juice
½   cup low-fat vanilla yogurt

1   cup frozen whole strawberries, thawed

1. Stir together orange juice and yogurt.

2. Process berries in a blender or food processor until smooth, stopping to scrape down sides. Stir into juice mixture. Spoon mixture into 12 (3-oz.) plastic pop molds; insert plastic pop sticks, and freeze 8 hours.

TO FREEZE IT: Keep pops frozen up to 3 months. If desired, place 12 (3-oz.) paper cups in a muffin pan. Spoon mixture evenly into cups. Freeze 30 minutes; insert a wooden craft stick into the center of each. Freeze 8 hours. Peel off cups.

Looks-Like-Watermelon Wedges: Hollow out lime halves, leaving rinds intact. Spoon pop mixture into lime rinds. Sprinkle with semisweet chocolate mini-morsels, and freeze 8 hours. Cut frozen lime halves in half with a bread knife to make wedges.

CREAMY PEANUT BUTTER JAMMIES

Makes: 24 squares   Hands-on Time: 30 min.   Total Time: 2 hr., 10 min.

1   (16.5-oz.) package refrigerated peanut butter cookie dough
1   (8-oz.) package cream cheese, softened
½   cup sugar
1   large egg
1   tsp. vanilla extract
⅓   cup seedless strawberry jam
⅓   cup chunky peanut butter
⅓   cup chopped roasted peanuts

1. Preheat oven to 325°. Line bottom and sides of an 11- x 7-inch baking dish with aluminum foil, allowing edges to extend 2 to 3 inches over sides. Lightly grease foil. Press two-thirds cookie dough evenly onto bottom.

2. Beat cream cheese and next 3 ingredients at medium speed with an electric mixer until smooth; spread evenly over cookie dough.

3. Stir together jam and peanut butter using a fork; dollop evenly over cream cheese mixture, being sure to include corners of pan. Gently swirl jam mixture and cream cheese mixture with a knife; crumble remaining cookie dough evenly over filling. Sprinkle with peanuts.

4. Bake at 325° for 40 to 45 minutes or until cream cheese layer is set and a wooden pick inserted in center comes out clean. Cool in pan on a wire rack 1 hour; chill in pan at least 30 minutes. Lift edges of foil, and remove from pan; gently peel off foil. Cut into 24 squares. Store in refrigerator. Remove from refrigerator 1 hour before serving.

TO FREEZE IT: Wrap the chilled jammies in plastic wrap, and wrap in foil. Label and freeze up to 3 weeks. To serve, thaw at room temperature.

do-ahead
desserts

WHITE FRUIT CAKE

Makes: 10 servings (2 loaves)   Hands-on Time: 25 min.   Total Time: 2 hrs., 6 min.

1 cup dark raisins	1 tsp. baking powder
1 cup golden raisins	½ tsp. salt
1 cup canned pineapple tidbits, drained	2 tsp. lemon zest
½ cup dried currants	2 tsp. orange zest
¼ cup orange juice	½ cup candied green cherries, quartered
1 cup butter, softened	¼ cup candied red cherries, quartered
1 cup sugar	Orange-Bourbon Glaze
5 large eggs	
2½ cups all-purpose flour	

1. Preheat oven to 325°. Stir together first 5 ingredients; cover and let stand 30 minutes.

2. Beat butter at medium speed with an electric mixer 2 minutes or until creamy. Gradually add sugar, beating 5 to 7 minutes or until blended. Add eggs, 1 at a time, beating just until yellow disappears.

3. Stir together flour, baking powder, and salt; reserve ½ cup flour mixture. Gradually add remaining flour mixture to butter mixture, beating at low speed just until blended after each addition. Stir in lemon and orange zest.

4. Drain raisin mixture, and stir in cherries. Toss raisin mixture with reserved ½ cup flour mixture, and fold into batter. Spoon batter into 2 lightly greased 8- x 4-inch loafpans.

5. Bake at 325° for 45 minutes to 1 hour or until a wooden pick inserted into center comes out clean. Brush hot cakes with Orange-Bourbon Glaze until absorbed. Cool in pans 10 minutes; invert cakes onto a wire rack, and cool completely.

 **TO FREEZE IT:** Wrap cake layers tightly with plastic wrap and loosely with aluminum foil. Label and freeze up to 1 month. Thaw at room temperature.

orange-bourbon glaze

Makes: ¼ cup   Hands-on Time: 5 min.   Total Time: 7 min.

¼ cup orange juice	2 Tbsp. bourbon
2 Tbsp. sugar	

1. Cook orange juice and sugar in a small saucepan over medium heat 2 minutes or until sugar is dissolved. Remove orange juice mixture from heat, and stir in bourbon.

CHOCOLATE-GINGER POUND CAKE

Makes: 12 servings   Hands-on Time: 12 min.   Total Time: 2 hr., 42 min.

- 1 (12-oz.) package semisweet chocolate morsels
- 1¼ cups butter, softened
- 2 cups sugar
- 5 large eggs
- 3 cups all-purpose flour
- 1 tsp. baking powder
- 1 tsp. ground ginger
- ⅛ tsp. salt
- 1 cup buttermilk
- ½ cup crystallized ginger, finely chopped
- 1 tsp. vanilla extract
- Garnishes: whipped cream, crystallized ginger

1. Preheat oven to 325°. Place chocolate morsels in a small microwave-safe glass bowl. Microwave at HIGH 1½ to 2 minutes or until melted and smooth, stirring at 30-second intervals.

2. Beat butter at medium speed with a heavy-duty electric stand mixer until creamy. Gradually add sugar, beating until light and fluffy. Add eggs, 1 at a time, beating just until yellow disappears. Add melted chocolate, beating just until blended.

3. Sift together flour and next 3 ingredients. Stir together buttermilk and crystallized ginger. Add flour mixture to butter mixture alternately with buttermilk mixture, beginning and ending with flour mixture. Beat at low speed just until blended after each addition. Stir in vanilla. Pour into a greased and floured 10-inch tube pan.

4. Bake at 325° for 1 hour and 10 minutes or until a long wooden pick inserted in center comes out clean. Cool in pan on a wire rack 10 minutes. Remove cake from pan to wire rack, and cool 1 hour or until completely cool. Garnish, if desired.

TO FREEZE IT: Wrap cooled cake tightly with plastic wrap. Wrap loosely with aluminum foil. Label and freeze up to 1 month. Thaw at room temperature.

It takes only six ingredients and two easy steps to create this from-scratch Southern staple. You'll need a heavy-duty stand mixer with a 4-qt. bowl and paddle attachment for this recipe.

TWO-STEP POUND CAKE

Makes: 10 to 12 servings   Hands-on Time: 15 min.   Total Time: 2 hr., 55 min.

- 4 cups all-purpose flour
- 3 cups sugar
- 2 cups butter, softened
- ¾ cup milk

- 6 large eggs
- 2 tsp. vanilla extract
- Garnish: powdered sugar

1. Preheat oven to 325°. Place flour, sugar, butter, milk, eggs, and vanilla (in that order) in 4-qt. bowl of a heavy-duty electric stand mixer. Beat at low speed 1 minute, stopping to scrape down sides. Beat at medium speed 2 minutes.

2. Pour batter into a greased and floured 10-inch (16-cup) tube pan, and smooth. Bake at 325° for 1 hour and 30 minutes or until a long wooden pick inserted in center comes out clean. Cool in pan on a wire rack 10 minutes. Remove from pan to wire rack, and cool completely (about 1 hour). Garnish, if desired.

TO FREEZE IT: Wrap cooled cake tightly with plastic wrap. Wrap loosely with aluminum foil. Label and freeze up to 1 month. Thaw at room temperature.

PECAN CAKE

Makes: 10 to 12 servings   Hands-on Time: 9 min.   Total Time: 3 hr.

2 cups butter, softened
1 (16-oz.) package light brown sugar
6 large eggs
3 Tbsp. instant coffee granules
3 Tbsp. hot water
½ cup milk

1 tsp. vanilla extract
4 ½ cups all-purpose flour
1 tsp. baking powder
¼ tsp. salt
4 cups chopped pecans

1. Preheat oven to 325°. Beat butter at medium speed with an electric mixer until creamy; gradually add brown sugar, beating well. Add eggs, 1 at a time, beating until blended after each addition.

2. Dissolve coffee granules in 3 Tbsp. hot water; stir in milk and vanilla.

3. Combine flour, baking powder, and salt; add to butter mixture alternately with milk mixture, beginning and ending with flour mixture. Beat at low speed until blended after each addition. Fold in pecans. Pour batter into a greased and floured 10-inch tube pan.

4. Bake at 325° for 1 hour and 30 minutes or until a wooden pick inserted in center comes out clean. Cool in pan on a wire rack 10 to 15 minutes; remove from pan, and cool completely on wire rack (about 1 hour).

TO FREEZE IT: Wrap cooled cake tightly with plastic wrap. Wrap loosely with aluminum foil. Label and freeze up to 1 month. Thaw at room temperature.

With the flavors of cinnamon, nutmeg, and ginger mixed with pecans and Granny Smith apples, this fresh dessert is good to the core.

APPLE BUNDT CAKE

Makes: 12 servings   Hands-on Time: 25 min.   Total Time: 3 hr., 40 min.

1 cup pecans, finely chopped
1½ cups sugar
1 cup canola oil
3 large eggs
1 tsp. vanilla extract
3 cups all-purpose flour
2 tsp. baking powder

1½ tsp. ground cinnamon
½ tsp. ground nutmeg
½ tsp. ground ginger
½ tsp. salt
4 cups (about 2 lb.) Granny Smith apples, peeled and diced

1. Preheat oven to 350°. Bake pecans in a single layer in a shallow pan 8 to 10 minutes or until toasted and fragrant, stirring halfway through.

2. Beat sugar and next 3 ingredients at high speed with a heavy-duty electric stand mixer 5 minutes. Stir together flour and next 5 ingredients; gradually add flour mixture to sugar mixture, beating at low speed just until blended. Add apples and pecans; beat just until blended. Spoon into a greased and floured 12-cup Bundt pan.

3. Bake at 350° for 1 hour to 1 hour and 10 minutes or until a long wooden pick inserted in center comes out clean. Cool in pan on a wire rack 15 minutes; remove from pan to wire rack, and cool completely (about 2 hours).

TO FREEZE IT: Wrap cooled cake tightly with plastic wrap. Wrap loosely with aluminum foil. Label and freeze up to 1 month. Thaw at room temperature.

SPICE CAKE WITH VANILLA-ORANGE BUTTERCREAM FROSTING

Make this cake ahead for the holidays or other special occasions.

Makes: 12 servings

Hands-on Time: 18 min.   Total Time: 2 hr., 40 min., including filling and frosting

1 cup chopped pecans	1½ cups buttermilk
1 cup butter, softened	1 tsp. vanilla extract
2 cups sugar	½ tsp. ground cinnamon
3 large eggs	½ tsp. ground allspice
3¼ cups all-purpose flour	¼ tsp. ground cloves
1 tsp. baking soda	Citrus Filling
½ tsp. salt	Vanilla-Orange Buttercream Frosting

1. Preheat oven to 350°. Bake pecans in a single layer in a shallow pan 5 to 7 minutes or until lightly toasted and fragrant, stirring halfway through. Let cool.

2. Meanwhile, beat butter at medium speed with a heavy-duty electric stand mixer until creamy. Gradually add sugar, beating until light and fluffy. Add eggs, 1 at a time, beating just until blended after each addition.

3. Stir together flour, baking soda, and salt; add to butter mixture alternately with buttermilk, beginning and ending with flour mixture. Beat at low speed just until blended after each addition. Stir in vanilla.

4. Divide batter into 2 equal portions (about 3½ cups each); stir cinnamon, allspice, cloves, and pecans into 1 portion. Pour plain batter into 2 greased and floured 9-inch round cake pans (about 1¾ cups batter per pan). Pour spiced batter into 2 greased and floured 9-inch round cake pans (about 2 cups batter per pan).

5. Bake at 350° for 18 to 20 minutes or until a wooden pick inserted in center comes out clean. Cool in pans on wire racks 10 minutes; remove from pans to wire racks, and cool completely (about 1 hour).

6. Place 1 plain cake layer on a serving plate or cake stand; spread top with ⅔ cup filling, leaving a ¼-inch border around edges. Top with a spice cake layer, and spread top with filling as directed above. Repeat procedure with remaining plain cake layer and filling. Top with remaining spice cake layer. Prepare Vanilla-Orange Buttercream Frosting; spread frosting over top and sides of cake.

TO FREEZE IT: Wrap cooled cake tightly with plastic wrap. Wrap loosely with aluminum foil. Label and freeze up to 1 month. Thaw in the fridge overnight.

citrus filling

Makes: about 2 cups   Hands-on Time: 5 min.   Total Time: 5 min.

2   (10-oz.) jars lemon curd
1½ cups sweetened flaked coconut
1   Tbsp. orange zest
1   Tbsp. fresh orange juice

1. Stir together lemon curd, coconut, and next 2 ingredients in a medium bowl until blended.

vanilla-orange buttercream frosting

Makes: about 2 cups   Hands-on Time: 5 min.   Total Time: 5 min

1   cup butter, softenend
3   Tbsp. orange zest
2   tsp. vanilla bean paste or vanilla extract
¼   tsp. salt
2   (16-oz) packages powdered sugar
4   to 5 Tbsp. milk

1. Beat first 4 ingredients at medium speed with an electric mixer until creamy.
2. Gradually add powdered sugar alternately with 3 Tbsp. milk, 1 Tbsp. at a time, beating at low speed until blended and smooth after each addition. Beat in up to 2 Tbsp. additional milk for desired consistency.

ORANGE CHIFFON CAKE

Makes: 12 to 16 servings
Hands-on Time: 45 min.   Total Time: 4 hr., 48 min., including filling and frosting

We used frozen orange juice concentrate scooped right out of the can in this cake's filling to deliver the greatest depth of flavor.

2½ cups sifted cake flour
1 Tbsp. baking powder
1 tsp. salt
1⅓ cups sugar
½ cup vegetable oil
5 large eggs, separated

¾ cup orange juice
3 Tbsp. orange zest
½ tsp. cream of tartar
Orange Icebox Pie Filling
Orange Buttercream Frosting
Garnish: orange zest

1. Preheat oven to 350°. Combine first 4 ingredients in a mixing bowl. Make a well in center of flour mixture; add oil, egg yolks, and orange juice. Beat at medium-high speed with an electric mixer 3 to 4 minutes or until smooth. Stir in zest.

2. Beat egg whites and cream of tartar at medium-high speed with an electric mixer until stiff peaks form. Gently fold into flour mixture. Spoon batter into 3 greased and floured 9-inch round cake pans.

3. Bake at 350° for 18 to 20 minutes or until a wooden pick inserted in center comes out clean. Cool in pans on wire racks 10 minutes; remove from pans, and cool completely on racks (about 1 hour).

4. Spread Orange Icebox Pie Filling between layers and on top of cake. Cover cake, and chill at least 4 hours. Spread Orange Buttercream Frosting around sides. Garnish, if desired.

TO FREEZE IT: Wrap assembled cake with plastic wrap, and cover with aluminum foil. Label and freeze up to 1 month. Thaw in fridge overnight.

orange icebox pie filling

Makes: about 3 cups   Hands-on Time: 13 min.   Total Time: 23 min.

¾ cup milk
¼ cup cornstarch
1 (14-oz.) can sweetened condensed milk
3 large eggs
½ cup thawed frozen orange juice concentrate

3 Tbsp. butter
2 drops red food coloring
4 drops yellow food coloring
1 Tbsp. fresh orange zest

1. Whisk together milk and cornstarch in a 3-quart heavy saucepan, whisking until cornstarch dissolves.

2. Whisk in condensed milk and eggs until blended; whisk in orange juice and food coloring. Bring to a boil over medium heat, whisking constantly. (Mixture will begin to thicken when orange juice is first added, and then become thin again during first few minutes of cooking. It will thicken quickly as it comes to a boil.)

3. Boil 1 minute, whisking constantly, or until mixture thickens. Remove from heat, and whisk in butter and orange zest until smooth. Pour filling into a large bowl, and place bowl in a larger bowl filled with ice. Stir regularly until cold (about 10 minutes).

orange buttercream frosting

Makes: 2½ cups   Hands-on Time: 10 min.   Total Time: 10 min.

½ cup butter, softened
1 (16-oz.) package powdered
   sugar, divided

⅓ cup milk
2 Tbsp. orange zest

1. Beat butter at medium speed with an electric mixer until creamy; gradually add 1 cup powdered sugar, beating at low speed until blended.

2. Add milk, beating until blended. Gradually add remaining powdered sugar, beating until blended. Stir in orange zest.

MINT CHOCOLATE CHIP ICE-CREAM CAKE

Makes: 10 to 12 servings   Hands-on Time: 30 min.   Total Time: 10 hr., 30 min.

Parchment paper
1   (18-oz.) box devil's food cake mix
½   gal. mint chocolate chip ice cream, softened
10   chocolate wafers, coarsely crushed
    Chocolate Ganache
    Garnish: thin crème de menthe chocolate mints

1. Preheat oven to 350°. Grease and flour 3 (8-inch) round cake pans. Line with parchment paper. Prepare cake mix according to package directions, and spoon into pans.

2. Bake at 350° for 12 to 14 minutes or until a wooden pick inserted in center comes out clean. Cool in pans on wire racks 10 minutes. Remove from pans to wire racks, peel off parchment paper, and cool completely (about 1 hour).

3. Place 1 cake layer in a 9-inch springform pan. Top with one-third of ice cream (about 2⅓ cups); sprinkle with half of crushed wafers. Repeat layers once. Top with remaining cake layer and ice cream. Freeze 8 to 12 hours.

TO FREEZE IT: Wrap assembled cake with plastic wrap and cover with aluminum foil. Label and freeze up to 1 month.

4. Remove cake from springform pan, and place on a cake stand or plate. Prepare Chocolate Ganache, and spread over top of ice-cream cake. Let stand 15 minutes before serving. Garnish, if desired.

chocolate ganache

Makes: ⅔ cup   Hands-on Time: 5 min.   Total Time: 5 min.

1   (4-oz.) semisweet chocolate baking bar, chopped
8   Tbsp. whipping cream

1. Microwave chocolate and 4 Tbsp. whipping cream in a microwave-safe bowl at HIGH 1 minute or until melted, stirring at 30-second intervals. Stir in up to 4 Tbsp. additional cream for desired consistency. Use immediately.

Note: Do not make ganache ahead.

Truly a mint-chocolate lover's dream: Layers of mint chocolate chip ice cream and devil's food chocolate cake are topped with a rich chocolate ganache.

Perfect for holiday gift giving, a swirl of chocolate and cream cheese drizzled with a powdered sugar icing takes this cake from ordinary to extraordinary.

CHOCOLATE-CREAM CHEESE COFFEE CAKE

Makes: 12 servings   **Hands-on Time: 30 min.**   **Total Time: 2 hr., 15 min.**

1⅓ cups all-purpose flour
½ cup firmly packed brown sugar
½ cup cold butter, cubed
1 cup chopped pecans
1 (8-oz.) package cream cheese, softened
¼ cup granulated sugar

1 Tbsp. flour
1 large egg
1 tsp. vanilla extract, divided
1 (1 lb., 3.5 oz.) box dark chocolate cake mix
1 cup powdered sugar
2 Tbsp. milk

1. Preheat oven to 350°. Stir together 1⅓ cups flour and brown sugar. Cut butter into mixture with a pastry blender or fork until crumbly; stir in pecans. Set aside. Beat cream cheese at medium speed with an electric mixer until smooth; add granulated sugar and 1 Tbsp. flour, beating until blended. Add egg and ½ tsp. vanilla, beating until blended.

2. Prepare cake mix according to package directions, and spoon into a lightly greased 13- x 9-inch baking pan. Dollop cream cheese mixture over batter, and gently swirl through cake batter with a knife. Sprinkle reserved pecan mixture over cake batter. Bake at 350° for 45 minutes or until set. Cool completely on a wire rack (1 hour).

TO FREEZE IT: Wrap tightly with aluminum foil. Label and freeze up to 1 month. Thaw partially at room temperature, and proceed with icing.

3. Whisk together powdered sugar, milk, and remaining ½ tsp. vanilla. Drizzle over tops of coffee cake.

BRANDY ALEXANDER CHEESECAKE

Makes: 10 to 12 servings   Hands-on Time: 20 min.   Total Time: 11 hr., 8 min.

1   (10-oz.) box chocolate-flavored
    bear-shaped graham crackers,
    crushed (about 2¼ cups)
6   Tbsp. butter, melted
2   Tbsp. sugar, divided
4   (8-oz.) packages cream cheese,
    softened
1¼ cups sugar

3   Tbsp. cornstarch
4   large eggs, at room temperature
4   Tbsp. brandy, divided
4   Tbsp. crème de cacao, divided*
1   (16-oz.) container sour cream
Garnishes: blackberries, raspberries,
    fresh mint

1. Preheat oven to 325°. Stir together crushed graham crackers, butter, and 1 Tbsp. sugar. Press mixture on bottom and halfway up sides of a 9-inch spring-form pan. Freeze 10 minutes.

2. Beat cream cheese, 1¼ cups sugar, and cornstarch at medium speed with an electric mixer 2 to 3 minutes or until smooth. Add eggs, 1 at a time, beating at low speed just until yellow disappears after each addition. Add 3 Tbsp. brandy and 3 Tbsp. crème de cacao, and beat just until blended. Pour into prepared crust.

3. Bake at 325° for 1 hour or just until center is almost set.

4. During last 2 minutes of baking, stir together sour cream and remaining 1 Tbsp. sugar, 1 Tbsp. brandy, and 1 Tbsp. crème de cacao.

5. Spread sour cream mixture over cheesecake. Bake at 325° for 8 more minutes. Remove cheesecake from oven; gently run a knife along outer edge of cheesecake, and cool completely in pan on a wire rack (about 1½ hours). Cover and chill 8 to 24 hours.

6. Remove sides of springform pan, and place cheesecake on a serving plate. Garnish, if desired.

*Coffee liqueur may be substituted. We tested with Kahlúa.

Note: We tested with Nabisco Teddy Grahams chocolate graham snacks.

TO FREEZE IT: Wrap springfrom pan tightly with aluminum foil, and slide into a zip-top plastic freezer bag; label and freeze up to 1 month. Thaw in the fridge overnight.

CHOCOLATE-MINT CUPCAKES

Makes: 2 dozen   Hands-on Time: 10 min.   Total Time: 1 hr., 45 min.

1   (18.25-oz.) package German
    chocolate cake mix
1   (16-oz.) container sour cream
¼   cup butter, melted
2   large eggs

1   tsp. vanilla extract
    Vegetable cooking spray
    Mint-Chocolate Buttercream Frosting
    Garnish: shaved thin crème de menthe
        chocolate mints

1. Preheat oven to 350°. Beat first 5 ingredients at low speed with an electric mixer just until dry ingredients are moistened. Increase speed to medium, and beat 3 to 4 minutes or until smooth, stopping to scrape bowl as needed.

2. Place paper baking cups in 12-cup muffin pans, and coat with cooking spray; spoon batter into baking cups, filling each two-thirds full.

3. Bake at 350° for 25 minutes or until a wooden pick inserted in center comes out clean. Cool in pans on wire racks 10 minutes; remove cupcakes from pans to wire racks, and cool 1 hour or until completely cool.

TO FREEZE IT: Wrap cupcakes tightly in foil, and place in a zip-top plastic freezer bag. Label and freeze up to 1 month. Thaw at room temperature.

4. Spread cupcakes with frosting. Garnish, if desired.

mint-chocolate buttercream frosting

Makes: 3 cups   Hands-on Time: 10 min.   Total Time: 10 min.

½   cup butter, softened
1   (3-oz.) package cream cheese,
    softened
1   (16-oz.) package powdered sugar

¼   cup milk
1   tsp. vanilla extract
¼   cup thin crème de menthe
    chocolate mints, finely chopped

1. Beat butter and cream cheese at medium speed with an electric mixer until creamy. Gradually add powdered sugar, beating at low speed until blended. Increase speed to medium, and slowly add milk and vanilla, beating until smooth. Stir in chocolate mints.

test kitchen tip

Pull a vegetable peeler along the edge of a thin chocolate mint to create the garnish.

LEMON MERINGUE ICE-CREAM PIE

Makes: 8 servings   Hands-on Time: 15 min.   Total Time: 11 hr., 25 min.

2   pt. vanilla ice cream
1   (6-oz.) package vanilla wafer crust
1½ cups Homemade Lemon Curd

4   vanilla wafers
2   cups whipped topping

1. Let ice cream stand at room temperature 5 minutes or just until soft enough to spread. Spoon 1 pt. ice cream into crust. Top with ¾ cup lemon curd; repeat with remaining ice cream and lemon curd. Gently swirl ice cream and curd with a knife or small spatula. Insert vanilla wafers around edge of pie. Cover and freeze 8 hours.

2. Dollop whipped topping over pie. Serve immediately, or cover loosely with plastic wrap, and freeze.

TO FREEZE IT: Wrap pie loosely with plastic wrap. Label and freeze up to 1 week. Thaw in fridge overnight.

homemade lemon curd

Makes: 2 cups   Hands-on Time: 30 min.   Total Time: 1 hr., 30 min.

2   cups sugar
½   cup butter, coarsely chopped
2   Tbsp. lemon zest

1   cup fresh lemon juice (about 6 lemons)
4   large eggs, lightly beaten

1. Stir together first 4 ingredients in a large heavy saucepan over medium heat, and cook, stirring constantly, 3 to 4 minutes or until sugar dissolves and butter melts.

2. Whisk about one-fourth of hot sugar mixture gradually into eggs; add egg mixture to remaining hot sugar mixture, whisking constantly. Cook over medium-low heat, whisking constantly, 15 minutes or until mixture thickens and coats back of a spoon. Remove from heat; cool completely (about 1 hour), stirring occasionally. Store in an airtight container in refrigerator up to 2 weeks.

This ultra-decadent chocolate pie recipe features a rich homemade chocolate pie filling topped with whipped cream and chopped chocolate candy bar pieces.

CHOCOLATE ICEBOX PIE

Makes: 8 servings   Hands-on Time: 28 min.   Total Time: 8 hr., 28 min.

⅔ cup milk
¾ cup semisweet chocolate morsels
¼ cup cold water
2 Tbsp. cornstarch
1 (14-oz.) can sweetened condensed milk
3 large eggs, beaten
1 tsp. vanilla extract

3 Tbsp. butter
1 (6-oz.) ready-made chocolate crumb piecrust
1 cup whipping cream
¼ cup sugar
½ cup chopped pecans, toasted
1 (1.55-oz.) milk chocolate candy bar, chopped

1. Heat milk in a 3-qt. saucepan over medium heat until it just begins to bubble around the edges (do not boil). Remove from heat, and whisk in chocolate morsels until melted. Cool slightly.

2. Stir together cold water and cornstarch until dissolved.

3. Whisk cornstarch mixture, sweetened condensed milk, eggs, and vanilla into chocolate mixture. Bring to a boil over medium heat, whisking constantly. Boil 1 minute or until mixture thickens and is smooth. (Do not overcook.)

4. Remove from heat, and whisk in butter. Spoon mixture into piecrust. Cover and chill at least 8 hours.

5. Beat whipping cream at high speed with an electric mixer until foamy; gradually add sugar, beating until soft peaks form. Dollop whipped cream over pie filling, and sprinkle with pecans and candy bar pieces.

TO FREEZE IT: Wrap pie tightly with plastic wrap, and cover with foil. Label and freeze up to 1 month.

MOCHA-PECAN MUD PIE

Makes: 9 servings   Hands-on Time: 15 min.   Total Time: 8 hr., 35 min.

½ cup chopped pecans
Vegetable cooking spray
1   tsp. sugar
1   pt. light coffee ice cream, softened
1   pt. light chocolate ice cream, softened

1   cup coarsely chopped reduced-fat cream-filled chocolate sandwich cookies, divided (about 10 cookies)
1   (6-oz.) ready-made chocolate crumb piecrust
2   Tbsp. light chocolate syrup

1. Preheat oven to 350°. Place pecans in a single layer on a baking sheet coated with cooking spray; sprinkle with sugar. Bake for 8 to 10 minutes or until lightly toasted, stirring halfway through. Cool.

2. Stir together ice creams, ¾ cup cookie chunks, and ⅓ cup pecans; spoon into piecrust. Freeze 10 minutes. Press remaining cookie chunks and pecans on top. Cover with plastic wrap, and freeze 8 hours.

TO FREEZE IT: Wrap tightly with plastic wrap; label and freeze up to 1 month.

3. Drizzle individual slices with chocolate syrup.

Note: We tested with Keebler Chocolate Ready Crust, Häagen-Dazs Light Coffee Ice Cream, and Häagen-Dazs Light Dutch Chocolate Ice Cream.

Make this pie even faster by making the chocolate crumb crust ahead. It can be frozen for up to 6 months.

CREAMY STRAWBERRY-MINT PIE

Makes: 10 servings   Hands-on Time: 30 min.   Total Time: 4 hr., 45 min.

16 reduced-fat cream-filled chocolate sandwich cookies
3   Tbsp. butter, melted
1   qt. fat-free or low-fat strawberry frozen yogurt
1   (16-oz.) package fresh strawberries, hulled

2   Tbsp. powdered sugar
2   Tbsp. chopped fresh mint
Garnishes: fresh strawberry slices, whipped topping, fresh mint

1. Preheat oven to 350°. Process cookies and butter in a food processor until finely chopped. Firmly press mixture on bottom and up sides of a lightly greased 9-inch springform pan. Bake 10 minutes. Cool completely on a wire rack (about 30 minutes).

2. Let frozen yogurt stand at room temperature 20 minutes or until slightly softened.

3. Process strawberries, powdered sugar, and mint in food processor until strawberries are pureed, stopping to scrape down sides as needed.

4. Place frozen yogurt in a large bowl; cut into large (3-inch) pieces. Fold strawberry mixture into yogurt until smooth. Spoon mixture into prepared crust. Freeze 3 hours or until firm.

TO FREEZE IT: Wrap pie tightly with plastic wrap; label and freeze up to 1 month.

5. Let stand at room temperature 15 minutes before serving. Garnish, if desired.

Note: We tested with Publix Low-Fat Strawberry Frozen Yogurt and Reduced-Fat Oreo cookies.

ORANGE CREAM PIE

Makes: 8 servings   Hands-on Time: 10 min.   Total Time: 8 hr., 10 min.

1 qt. ice cream, softened
1 (11-oz.) can mandarin orange
   segments, drained
1 (6-oz.) reduced-fat graham
   cracker crust

Orange Glaze (optional)
Garnish: mandarin orange segments

1. Beat softened ice cream and mandarin oranges at medium speed with an electric mixer until blended. Spoon into piecrust. Cover and freeze 8 hours or until firm.

TO FREEZE IT: Wrap pie tightly with plastic wrap; label and freeze up to 1 month.

2. Serve with Orange Glaze, if desired. Garnish, if desired.

orange glaze

Makes: 1 cup   Hands-on Time: 5 min.   Total Time: 2 hr., 7 min.

⅔ cup sugar
2 Tbsp. cornstarch
3 Tbsp. orange liqueur
1 Tbsp. orange zest

2½ Tbsp. light corn syrup
2 drops red food coloring
3 drops yellow food coloring

1. Bring all ingredients and ⅓ cup water to a boil in a small saucepan, stirring constantly; boil 2 minutes. Cover glaze, and chill 2 hours.

test kitchen tip
For neat pieces, run a knife under hot water for 1 minute before slicing.

FRIED STRAWBERRY PIES

Makes: 18 pies   Hands-on Time: 48 min.   Total Time: 1 hr., 48 min.

2   cups fresh strawberries, mashed
¾   cup sugar
¼   cup cornstarch
1   (14.1-oz.) package refrigerated
    piecrusts

Vegetable oil
Powdered sugar

1. Combine first 3 ingredients in a saucepan. Bring strawberry mixture to a boil over medium heat. Cook, stirring constantly, 1 minute or until thickened. Cool completely.

2. Roll 1 piecrust to press out fold lines; cut into 9 circles with a 3-inch round cutter. Roll circles to 3½-inch diameter; moisten edges with water. Spoon 2 tsp. strawberry mixture in the center of each circle; fold over, pressing edges to seal. Repeat with remaining piecrust and strawberry mixture.

3. Place pies in a single layer on a baking sheet, and freeze at least 1 hour.

TO FREEZE IT: Place pies in a zip-top plastic freezer bag; label and freeze up to 1 month. To prepare, proceed with recipe as directed.

4. Pour oil to a depth of 1 inch in a large heavy skillet; heat to 350°. Fry pies, in batches, 1 minute on each side or until golden. Drain on paper towels; sprinkle with powdered sugar.

test kitchen tip

Freezing the pies before frying them prevents the crusts from disintegrating in hot oil.

Look for parchment paper in kitchen stores or in the plastic wrap aisle of the supermarket. If you can't find parchment, coat aluminum foil with vegetable cooking spray; then press the coated side against the piecrust.

TANGY LEMON TART

Makes: 8 to 10 servings   Hands-on Time: 9 min.   Total Time: 4 hr., 47 min.

½ (14.1-oz.) package refrigerated piecrusts
1 Tbsp. coarse sparkling sugar

Tangy Lemon Tart Filling
Garnishes: whipping cream, blueberries, lemon zest curls

1. Preheat oven to 425°. Unfold piecrust on a lightly floured surface. Fit piecrust into the bottom and up sides of a 9-inch tart pan (about 1½ to 1¾ inches deep). Prick bottom of crust with a fork. Freeze 10 minutes.

2. Line piecrust with parchment paper; fill with pie weights or dried beans.

3. Bake at 425° for 10 minutes. Remove weights and parchment paper; sprinkle crust with sugar, and bake 12 to 15 more minutes or until lightly browned.

4. Pour Tangy Lemon Tart Filling into crust; cover and chill 4 hours or until set. Garnish, if desired.

tangy lemon tart filling

Makes: 1 cup   Hands-on Time: 22 min.   Total Time: 32 min.

1 cup sugar
3 Tbsp. cornstarch
½ cup fresh lemon juice (about 4 large lemons)*

4 large eggs, lightly beaten
¼ cup butter, melted
2 drops liquid yellow food coloring

1. Whisk together sugar and cornstarch in a heavy nonaluminum saucepan; gradually whisk in lemon juice, eggs, and butter. Cook mixture, whisking constantly, over medium-low heat 8 to 12 minutes or until thick and bubbly. Remove from heat, add food coloring, and let stand 10 minutes.

*½ cup thawed lemon juice may be substituted.

TO FREEZE IT: Wrap pie tightly with plastic wrap, and cover with aluminum foil. Label and freeze up to 1 week. Thaw in the fridge overnight.

test kitchen tip

Shield the outside edges of the pie crust with aluminum foil to prevent excessive browning.

CHOCOLATE COFFEE CHEESECAKE TRUFFLES

Makes: 15 tartlets   Hands-on Time: 30 min.   Total Time: 2 hr., 38 min.

2 Tbsp. slivered almonds	1 (3-oz.) package cream cheese, softened
1 (2.1-oz.) package frozen mini-phyllo pastry shells, thawed	3 Tbsp. powdered sugar
2 Tbsp. heavy cream, divided	2 Tbsp. light brown sugar
½ tsp. instant espresso powder	1 oz. bittersweet chocolate

1. Preheat oven to 350°. Place almonds in a single layer in a shallow pan. Bake at 350°, stirring occasionally, 5 to 7 minutes or until lightly toasted and fragrant.

2. Place thawed pastry shells on a baking sheet, and bake at 350° for 3 to 5 minutes or until crisp.

3. Stir together 1 Tbsp. cream and espresso powder in a small microwave-safe ramekin or cup. Microwave at HIGH 10 seconds; stir until espresso is dissolved.

4. Beat cream cheese and sugars at medium-high speed with an electric mixer until smooth. Gradually add espresso mixture, and beat 30 seconds or until creamy and light. Spoon 1 rounded teaspoonful into each phyllo shell.

5. Microwave chocolate and remaining 1 Tbsp. cream in a small microwave-safe ramekin or cup at HIGH 20 seconds, stirring after 10 seconds and at end until smooth. Spoon ¼ tsp. chocolate mixture over each tart.

TO FREEZE IT: Save the plastic tart shell packaging to store the prepared tartlets. Wrap tightly with plastic wrap, and freeze up to 1 week. Freeze the toasted almonds separately, adding them after frozen. Thaw in fridge overnight.

6. Top immediately with almonds. Cover and chill 2 hours or up to 24 hours.

TINY CARAMEL TARTS

Makes: 6 dozen

Hands-on Time: 30 min.   Total Time: 4 hr., 30 min., including pastry shells

2 cups sugar, divided
½ cup cold butter, sliced
6 Tbsp. all-purpose flour
4 egg yolks

2 cups milk
Cream Cheese Pastry Shells (page 30)
Garnish: chopped candies and nuts

1. Cook 1 cup sugar in a medium-size heavy skillet over medium heat, stirring constantly, 6 to 8 minutes or until sugar melts and turns golden brown. Stir in butter until melted.

2. Whisk together flour, egg yolks, milk, and remaining 1 cup sugar in a 3-qt. heavy saucepan; bring just to a simmer over low heat, whisking constantly. Add sugar mixture to flour mixture, and cook, whisking constantly, 1 to 2 minutes or until thickened. Cover and chill 4 hours.

3. Meanwhile, prepare Cream Cheese Pastry Shells. Spoon caramel mixture into pastry shells.

TO FREEZE IT: Place the tarts in an airtight container, and freeze up to 1 week. Thaw in fridge overnight.

4. Garnish, if desired.

FROSTED SUGAR 'N' SPICE COOKIES

Makes: 2½ dozen   Hands-on Time: 1 hr.   Total Time: 3 hr., 43 min.

- 2 cups all-purpose flour
- 1 tsp. baking powder
- ½ tsp. baking soda
- ½ tsp. ground cinnamon
- ¼ tsp. salt
- ⅛ tsp. ground nutmeg
- ⅓ cup butter, softened
- ½ cup granulated sugar
- ½ cup firmly packed brown sugar
- 2 egg yolks
- 5 oz. cream cheese, softened
- 1 tsp. orange zest
- 1 tsp. vanilla extract
- Simple White Frosting
- Colored sugar

1. Stir together first 6 ingredients in a bowl.

2. Beat butter and next 3 ingredients at medium speed with an electric mixer until creamy. Add cream cheese, orange zest, and vanilla; beat until well blended. Gradually add flour mixture, beating at low speed until blended.

3. Divide dough in half, shaping into 2 flattened disks. Cover with plastic wrap, and chill 2 to 24 hours.

4. Preheat oven to 350°. Place 1 dough disk on a floured surface. Roll to ¼-inch thickness; cut with a 4-inch star-shaped cutter. Place 1 inch apart on ungreased baking sheets. Repeat procedure with remaining dough disk.

5. Bake at 350° for 8 to 10 minutes or just until edges are lightly browned. Cool on baking sheets 3 minutes. Transfer to a wire rack, and let cool 30 minutes or until completely cool.

 **TO FREEZE IT:** Freeze cookies in a labeled zip-top plastic freezer bag up to 1 month. Thaw completely at room temperature before frosting.

6. Spread cookies with a thin layer of Simple White Frosting; top with colored sugar.

simple white frosting

Makes: about 1½ cups   Hands-on Time: 10 min.   Total Time: 10 min.

- ¼ cup butter, softened
- ⅛ tsp. salt
- 3 cups powdered sugar, divided
- 4 Tbsp. milk, divided

1. Beat butter, salt, 1½ cups powdered sugar, and 3 Tbsp. milk at medium speed with an electric mixer until blended. Gradually beat in remaining powdered sugar and milk.

SPICE COOKIES

Makes: about 4 dozen   Hands-on Time: 30 min.   Total Time: 2 hr., 40 min.

1¾ cups sugar, divided
1   cup butter, softened
2   large eggs
1   Tbsp. milk
4   cups all purpose flour
1½ tsp. baking soda

1½ tsp. ground cinnamon
½   tsp. ground nutmeg
¼   tsp. ground cloves
1   cup dried currants or raisins
Orange Glaze

1. Beat 1½ cups sugar and butter at medium speed with an electric mixer until smooth. Add eggs, beating 1 at a time, until blended. Add milk; beat at low speed until blended.

2. Combine flour and next 4 ingredients; gradually add to butter mixture, beating until blended. Stir in currants. Shape dough into a ball; wrap in plastic wrap, and chill 2 hours.

TO FREEZE IT: Place wrapped cookies in a zip-top plastic freezer bag; label and freeze up to 1 month. Thaw in fridge overnight.

3. Preheat oven to 350°. Turn dough out onto a lightly floured surface, and roll to ⅛-inch thickness; sprinkle top with remaining ¼ cup sugar. Cut dough with a 2½-inch round or other desired shape cutter. Place 2 inches apart on baking sheets.

4. Bake at 350° for 8 to 10 minutes or until lightly browned. Cool on baking sheets 3 to 4 minutes. Remove to wire racks, and let cool completely. Drizzle Orange Glaze over cookies.

orange glaze

Makes: ½ cup   Hands-on Time: 10 min.   Total Time: 10 min.

1   cup powdered sugar
1   tsp. orange zest

¼   cup fresh orange juice

1. Stir together all ingredients until smooth.

PEPPERMINT PINWHEEL COOKIES

Makes: 4 dozen   Hands-on Time: 35 min.   Total Time: 5 hr., 17 min.

½ cup butter, softened
1 cup sugar
1 large egg
½ tsp. vanilla extract
1¾ cups all-purpose flour

½ tsp. baking soda
¼ tsp. salt
¾ tsp. red food coloring paste
Parchment paper
Peppermint Frosting

1. Beat butter at medium speed with a heavy-duty electric stand mixer until creamy; gradually add sugar, beating until light and fluffy. Add egg and vanilla, beating until blended, scraping bowl as needed.

2. Combine flour, baking soda, and salt; gradually add flour mixture to butter mixture, beating at low speed until blended.

3. Divide dough into 2 equal portions. Roll 1 portion of dough into a 12- x 8-inch rectangle on a piece of lightly floured plastic wrap.

4. Knead food coloring paste into remaining portion of dough while wearing rubber gloves. Roll tinted dough into a rectangle as directed in Step 3. Invert untinted dough onto tinted dough; peel off plastic wrap. Cut dough in half lengthwise, forming 2 (12- x 4-inch) rectangles. Roll up each rectangle, jelly-roll fashion, starting at 1 long side, using bottom piece of plastic wrap as a guide. Wrap in plastic wrap, and freeze 4 hours.

TO FREEZE IT: Label and freeze cookie dough in plastic wrap up to 1 month. Proceed with recipe as directed.

5. Preheat oven to 350°. Cut ends off each dough log, and discard. Cut dough into ¼-inch-thick pieces, and place on parchment paper-lined baking sheets.

6. Bake at 350° for 6 to 7 minutes or until puffed and set; cool cookies on baking sheets 5 minutes. Remove to wire racks, and cool completely (about 30 minutes).

7. Place Peppermint Frosting in a heavy-duty zip-top plastic freezer bag. Snip 1 corner of bag to make a small hole. Pipe about 2 tsp. frosting onto half of cookies; top with remaining cookies, gently pressing to form a sandwich.

Note: These cookies are delicious eaten at room temperature, or chill them 30 minutes for a firm, cool filling.

peppermint frosting

Makes: 1¾ cups   Hands-on Time: 10 min.   Total Time: 10 min.

¼   cup butter, softened
1   (3-oz.) package cream
     cheese, softened

2   cups powdered sugar
1   Tbsp. milk
⅛   tsp. peppermint extract

1. Beat butter and cream cheese at medium speed with an electric mixer until creamy. Gradually add powdered sugar, beating at low speed until blended. Increase speed to medium, and gradually add milk and peppermint extract, beating until smooth.

SLICE-AND-BAKE SHORTBREAD COOKIES

Makes: 4 dozen   Hands-on Time: 15 min.   Total Time: 5 hr., 15 min.

Stock your freezer with this simple dough for cookies in a jiffy. You'll be ready to slice and bake in minutes.

1 cup butter, softened	2 cups all-purpose flour
¾ cup powdered sugar	¼ tsp. baking powder
2 tsp. vanilla extract	⅛ tsp. salt
½ tsp. almond extract	Wax paper

1. Beat butter at medium speed with an electric mixer until creamy. Gradually add powdered sugar, beating until smooth. Stir in vanilla and almond extract until blended.

2. Stir together flour, baking powder, and salt.

3. Gradually add flour mixture to butter mixture, beating at low speed until blended.

4. Shape shortbread dough into 2 (7-inch) logs. Wrap each log in wax paper, and chill 4 hours.

TO FREEZE IT: Freeze logs in labeled zip-top plastic freezer bags up to 1 month. Let stand at room temperature 10 minutes before proceeding with directions in Step 5.

5. Preheat oven to 350°.

6. Cut each log into 24 slices. Place shortbread slices 1 inch apart on lightly greased or parchment paper-lined baking sheets.

7. Bake shortbread slices at 350° for 10 to 12 minutes or until edges of slices are golden.

8. Remove shortbread from baking sheets, and place on wire racks; let cool completely (about 20 minutes). Store in airtight containers.

Cranberry-Orange Shortbread Cookies: Stir in ½ cup chopped dried cranberries and 1 Tbsp. orange zest with extracts in Step 1.

Pecan Shortbread Cookies: Omit almond extract. Stir in 1 cup finely chopped toasted pecans with vanilla in Step 1.

Toffee-Espresso Shortbread Cookies: Omit almond extract. Stir in ½ cup toffee bits and 1 Tbsp. espresso powder with vanilla in Step 1.

Coconut-Macadamia Nut Shortbread Cookies: Omit almond extract. Stir in 1 cup toasted coconut, ½ cup finely chopped macadamia nuts, and ¼ tsp. coconut extract with vanilla in Step 1.

WHITE CHOCOLATE-COVERED PRETZEL COOKIES

Makes: about 5 dozen   Hands-on Time: 30 min.   Total Time: 59 min.

- ¾ cup butter, softened
- ¾ cup granulated sugar
- ¾ cup firmly packed dark brown sugar
- 2 large eggs
- 1½ tsp. vanilla extract
- 2¼ cups plus 2 Tbsp. all-purpose flour
- 1 tsp. baking soda
- ¾ tsp. salt
- 1½ (12-oz.) packages semisweet chocolate morsels
- 1 (5-oz.) bag white chocolate-covered mini pretzel twists, coarsely crushed
- Parchment paper

1. Preheat oven to 350°. Beat butter and sugars at medium speed with a heavy-duty electric stand mixer until creamy. Add eggs and vanilla, beating until blended.

2. Combine flour, baking soda, and salt in a small bowl; gradually add to butter mixture, beating just until blended. Beat in morsels and pretzel twists just until combined. Drop by tablespoonfuls onto parchment paper-lined baking sheets.

3. Bake at 350° for 10 to 14 minutes or until desired degree of doneness. Remove to wire racks, and cool completely (about 15 minutes).

TO FREEZE IT: Place cookies in an airtight container or zip-top plastic freezer bag; label and freeze up to 3 months. Thaw at room temperature.

BLUEBERRY-PECAN SHORTBREAD SQUARES

Makes: 2 dozen   Hands-on Time: 20 min.   Total Time: 3 hr., 18 min.

¾ cup chopped pecans
2¼ cups all-purpose flour
½ tsp. salt
1 cup butter, softened
1½ cups powdered sugar

¼ tsp. vanilla extract
3 (4.4-oz.) containers fresh
   blueberries (about 2½ cups)
2 Tbsp. granulated sugar
1 tsp. lime zest

1. Preheat oven to 350°. Place pecans in a single layer in a shallow pan. Bake at 350° for 8 minutes or until toasted and fragrant, stirring halfway through.

2. Stir together pecans, flour, and salt in a bowl.

3. Beat butter and powdered sugar at medium speed with a heavy-duty electric stand mixer 2 minutes or until pale and fluffy. Beat in vanilla. Gradually add flour mixture, beating at low speed 30 seconds after each addition until a dough froms and comes together to hold a shape.

4. Press 2 cups of dough in a thick layer onto bottom of a lightly greased 13- x 9-inch pan. Top with fresh blueberries. Combine granulated sugar and lime zest, and sprinkle over berries. Crumble remaining dough over berries.

5. Bake at 350° for 45 to 50 minutes or until golden. Cool shortbread in pan on a wire rack 2 hours. Cut into squares before serving.

TO FREEZE IT: Once cooled, place in single layer in a zip-top plastic freezer bag or airtight container with wax paper between the layers. Label and freeze up to 3 months. Thaw at room temperature.

BROWNIE BUTTONS

Makes: 24 brownies   Hands-on Time: 15 min.   Total Time: 47 min.

1 (18.9-oz.) package Triple Chunk
   Brownie mix

1 bag assorted miniature peanut
   butter cup candies and
   chocolate-coated caramels

1. Preheat oven to 350°. Prepare brownie mix according to package directions. Spray miniature muffin pans with cooking spray, or line pans with paper liners, and spray liners with cooking spray. Spoon brownie batter into each cup, filling almost full. Bake at 350° for 19 to 20 minutes. Cool in pans 3 to 4 minutes, and then gently press a miniature candy into each baked brownie until the top of candy is level with top of brownie. Cool 10 minutes in pans. Gently twist each brownie to remove from pan. Cool on a wire rack.

TO FREEZE IT: Let brownies cool completely. Place in a zip-top plastic freezer bag; label and freeze up to 3 months. Thaw at room temperature.

SIMPLE BROWNIES WITH CHOCOLATE FROSTING

Makes: about 4 dozen
Hands-on Time: 15 min.   Total Time: 1 hr., 56 min., including frosting

1½ cups coarsely chopped pecans	2 cups sugar
1 (4-oz.) unsweetened chocolate baking bar, chopped	4 large eggs
¾ cup butter	1 cup all-purpose flour
	Chocolate Frosting

1. Preheat oven to 350°. Bake pecans in a single layer in a shallow pan 6 to 8 minutes or until lightly toasted and fragrant, stirring halfway through.

2. Microwave chocolate and butter in a large microwave-safe bowl at HIGH 1 to 1½ minutes or until melted and smooth, stirring at 30-second intervals. Whisk in sugar and eggs until well blended. Stir in flour. Spread batter into a greased 13- x 9-inch pan.

3. Bake at 350° for 25 to 30 minutes or until a wooden pick inserted in center comes out with a few moist crumbs.

4. Meanwhile, prepare Chocolate Frosting. Pour over warm brownies; spread to edges. Sprinkle with pecans. Let cool 1 hour on a wire rack. Cut into squares.

TO FREEZE IT: Let brownies cool completely. Place frosted brownies in a zip-top plastic freezer bag; label and freeze up to 3 months. Thaw at room temperature.

chocolate frosting

Makes: 2 cups   Hands-on Time: 10 min.   Total Time: 10 min.

½ cup butter	1 (16-oz.) package powdered sugar
⅓ cup milk	1 tsp. vanilla extract
6 Tbsp. unsweetened cocoa	

1. Cook first 3 ingredients in a large saucepan over medium heat, stirring constantly, 4 to 5 minutes or until butter melts. Remove from heat, and beat in powdered sugar and vanilla at medium speed with an electric mixer until smooth.

PECAN-PEACH COBBLER

Makes: 8 to 10 servings   Hands-on Time: 40 min.   Total Time: 1 hr., 40 min.

12 to 15 fresh peaches, peeled and sliced (about 16 cups)

3 cups sugar

⅓ cup all-purpose flour

½ tsp. nutmeg

⅔ cup butter

1½ tsp. vanilla

2 (14.1-oz.) packages refrigerated piecrusts

½ cup chopped pecans, toasted

¼ cup sugar

1. Preheat oven to 475°. Combine first 4 ingredients in a Dutch oven, and let stand 10 minutes or until sugar dissolves. Bring peach mixture to a boil; reduce heat to low, and simmer 10 minutes or until tender. Remove from heat; add butter and vanilla, stirring until butter melts.

2. Unfold 2 piecrusts. Sprinkle ¼ cup pecans and 2 Tbsp. sugar over 1 piecrust; top with other piecrust. Roll into a 12-inch circle, gently pressing pecans into pastry. Cut into 1½-inch strips. Repeat with remaining piecrusts, pecans, and sugar.

3. Spoon half of peach mixture into a lightly greased 13- x 9-inch baking dish. Arrange half of pastry strips in a lattice design over top of peach mixture.

4. Bake at 475° for 20 to 25 minutes or until lightly browned. Spoon remaining peach mixture over baked pastry. Top with remaining pastry strips in a lattice design. Bake 15 to 18 more minutes. Serve warm or cold.

TO FREEZE IT: Let cobbler cool completely. Cover tightly with plastic wrap and aluminum foil; label and freeze up to 1 month. Thaw in fridge overnight. Uncover and reheat in the oven at 250° for 45 minutes.

PEACH-PECAN RUGELACH

Makes: about 5 dozen   Hands-on Time: 1 hr., 15 min.   Total Time: 4 hr., 50 min.

1   cup chopped pecans
2¼ cups all-purpose flour
1   cup butter, cut into pieces
1   (8-oz.) package cream cheese, cut
    into pieces

½   tsp. salt
1   (12-oz.) jar peach preserves
Parchment paper
3   Tbsp. sugar
2   tsp. ground cinnamon

1. Preheat oven to 350°. Bake pecans in a single layer in a shallow pan 10 to 12 minutes or until toasted and fragrant, stirring halfway through.

2. Pulse flour and next 3 ingredients in a food processor 3 or 4 times until dough forms a small ball and leaves sides of bowl. Divide dough into 2 portions, shaping each portion into a ball. Wrap each ball separately in plastic wrap, and chill 1 to 24 hours.

3. Heat preserves in a small saucepan over medium heat, stirring often, 2 to 3 minutes or until warm.

4. Roll 1 dough ball onto lighlty floured parchment paper into a 17- x 12-inch rectangle. Spread with half of peach preserves and half of pecans. Roll up, beginning on wide side, using parchment paper as a guide. Repeat with remaining dough ball. Wrap in plastic wrap, and freeze at least 2 hours.

TO FREEZE IT: Place wrapped dough rolls in a zip-top plastic freezer bag; label and freeze up to 1 month.

5. Preheat oven to 375°. Slice dough rolls into ⅓-inch-thick slices. Arrange on lightly greased parchment paper-lined baking sheets. Combine sugar and cinnamon; sprinkle over slices.

6. Bake at 375° for 15 to 20 minutes or until golden. Remove from baking sheets, and transfer to wire racks. Cool completely (about 20 minutes).

Apricot-Almond Rugelach: Substitute apricot preserves for peach preserves and almonds for pecans. Prepare recipe as directed, decreasing toasting time in Step 1 to 8 to 10 minutes.

PEANUTTY ICE-CREAM SANDWICHES

Makes: 9 servings   Hands-on Time: 20 min.   Total Time: 2 hr., 6 min.

⅔ cup butter
2   cups quick-cooking oats, uncooked
¾ cup firmly packed dark brown sugar
½ cup finely chopped dry-roasted peanuts
1   large egg, lightly beaten
¼ cup all-purpose flour
¼ tsp. baking powder
¼ tsp. salt
1   tsp. vanilla extract
Parchment paper
½ cup chunky peanut butter
3   cups vanilla ice cream, softened
1   cup coarsely chopped dry-roasted peanuts

1. Preheat oven to 350°. Melt butter in a Dutch oven over medium heat. Remove from heat, and stir in oats and next 7 ingredients.

2. Drop oat mixture by tablespoonfuls 3 inches apart onto a parchment paper-lined baking sheet. Spread each dollop of cookie batter to form a 3-inch circle.

3. Bake at 350° for 9 to 11 minutes or until edges are golden. Remove from pan, and cool completely on a wire rack.

4. Swirl peanut butter into softened ice cream. Freeze 30 minutes. Scoop ice cream evenly on flat sides of half of cookies; top with remaining cookies, flat sides down. Roll sides of sandwiches in coarsely chopped peanuts. Place in plastic or wax paper sandwich bags, and freeze at least 1 hour.

Note: Do not substitute a greased baking sheet for parchment paper. Cookies will slide and tear.

TO FREEZE IT: Place ice-cream sandwiches in a zip-top plastic freezer bag and freeze up to 2 weeks.

WATERMELON GRANITA

Makes: about 7 cups   Hands-on Time: 20 min.   Total Time: 8 hr., 35 min.

8   cups seeded and cubed watermelon   1½ cups lemon-lime soft drink
1   (6-oz.) can frozen orange juice
       concentrate, thawed

1. Process watermelon in a blender or food processor until smooth.

2. Stir together watermelon puree and remaining ingredients. Pour mixture into a 2-qt. glass bowl. Cover and freeze 8 hours, stirring occasionally.

TO FREEZE IT: Freeze in a labeled airtight container up to 2 weeks.

3. Remove from freezer 15 minutes before serving. Stir with a fork, and spoon into glasses. Serve immediately.

Note: We tested with 7UP soft drink.

STRAWBERRY-BUTTERMILK SHERBET

Makes: about 4½ cups   Hands-on Time: 15 min.   Total Time: 3 hr., 15 min.

2   cups fresh strawberries*
2   cups buttermilk
1   cup sugar

1   tsp. vanilla extract
Garnish: fresh mint sprigs

1. Process strawberries in a food processor or blender 30 seconds or until smooth, stopping to scrape down sides. Pour strawberry puree through a fine wire-mesh strainer into a large bowl, pressing with back of a spoon. Discard solids. Add buttermilk, sugar, and vanilla to puree; stir until well blended. Cover and chill 1 hour.

2. Pour strawberry mixture into freezer container of a 1½-qt. electric ice-cream maker, and freeze according to manufacturer's instructions. Garnish, if desired.

*1 (16-oz.) package frozen strawberries, thawed, may be substituted.

TO FREEZE IT: Place sherbet in an airtight container; label and freeze up to 1 month.

MOCHA LATTE ICE CREAM

Makes: about 1 qt.

Hands-on Time: 20 min.   Total Time: 9 hr., 20 min., not including freezing time

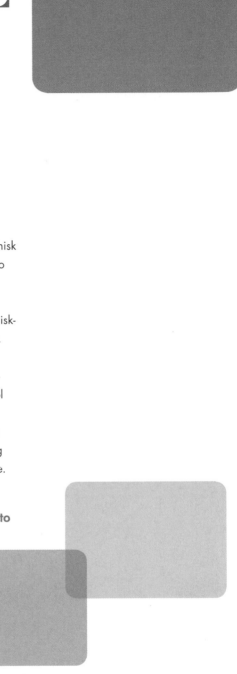

- ¾ cup sugar
- 2 Tbsp. cornstarch
- 1 Tbsp. instant espresso
- ⅛ tsp. salt
- 2 cups milk
- 1 cup heavy whipping cream
- 1 egg yolk
- 1½ tsp. vanilla bean paste or vanilla extract
- 1 cup chopped pecans
- 2 oz. finely chopped semisweet chocolate
- Garnish: cream-filled rolled wafer cookies

1. Whisk together first 4 ingredients in a large heavy saucepan. Gradually whisk in milk and whipping cream. Cook over medium heat, stirring constantly, 10 to 12 minutes or until mixture thickens slightly. Remove from heat.

2. Whisk egg yolk until slightly thickened. Gradually whisk about 1 cup hot cream mixture into yolk. Add yolk mixture to remaining hot cream mixture, whisking constantly. Whisk in vanilla bean paste. Cool 1 hour, stirring occasionally.

3. Place plastic wrap directly on cream mixture, and chill 8 to 24 hours.

4. Meanwhile, preheat oven to 350°. Bake pecans in a single layer in a shallow pan 8 minutes or until toasted and fragrant, stirring halfway through. Cool completely (about 30 minutes).

5. Pour chilled cream mixture into freezer container of a 1½-qt. electric ice-cream maker, and freeze according to manufacturer's instructions. Before transferring ice cream to an airtight container for further freezing, stir in pecans and chocolate. Garnish, if desired.

TO FREEZE IT: Place ice cream in an airtight container; label and freeze up to 1 month.

CHERRY BOURBON ICE CREAM

Makes: about 1 qt. (serving size ½ cup)
Hands-on Time: 20 min.   Total Time: 9 hr., 20 min.

½ cup granular sweetener for ice cream*

2 Tbsp. cornstarch

⅛ tsp. salt

2 cups 2% reduced-fat milk

1 cup half-and-half

1 egg yolk

1½ tsp. vanilla bean paste or vanilla extract

½ cup drained and coarsely chopped canned, pitted cherries in heavy syrup

3 Tbsp. bourbon

1. Whisk together first 3 ingredients in a large heavy saucepan. Gradually whisk in milk and half-and-half. Cook over medium heat, stirring constantly, 8 to 10 minutes or until mixture thickens slightly. Remove from heat.

2. Whisk egg yolk until slightly thickened. Gradually whisk about 1 cup hot cream mixture into yolk. Add yolk mixture to remaining hot cream mixture, whisking constantly. Whisk in vanilla.

3. Pour mixture through a fine wire-mesh strainer into a bowl, discarding solids. Cool 1 hour, stirring occasionally. Place plastic wrap directly on cream mixture; chill 8 to 24 hours.

4. Pour mixture into freezer container of a 1½-qt. electric ice-cream maker, and freeze according to manufacturer's instructions; stir in cherries and bourbon halfway through freezing.

TO FREEZE IT: Place ice cream in an airtight container; label and freeze up to 1 month.

5. Let stand at room temperature 5 to 10 minutes before serving.
*Granulated sugar may be substituted.

Note: We tested with Whey Low 100% All Natural Granular Sweetener for Ice Cream.

metric equivalents

The recipes that appear in this cookbook use the standard U.S. method for measuring liquid and dry or solid ingredients (teaspoons, tablespoons, and cups). The information in the following charts is provided to help cooks outside the United States successfully use these recipes. All equivalents are approximate.

Metric Equivalents for Different Types of Ingredients

A standard cup measure of a dry or solid ingredient will vary in weight depending on the type of ingredient. A standard cup of liquid is the same volume for any type of liquid. Use the following chart when converting standard cup measures to grams (weight) or milliliters (volume).

Standard Cup	Fine Powder (ex. flour)	Grain (ex. rice)	Granular (ex. sugar)	Liquid Solids (ex. butter)	Liquid (ex. milk)
1	140 g	150 g	190 g	200 g	240 ml
¾	105 g	113 g	143 g	150 g	180 ml
⅔	93 g	100 g	125 g	133 g	160 ml
½	70 g	75 g	95 g	100 g	120 ml
⅓	47 g	50 g	63 g	67 g	80 ml
¼	35 g	38 g	48 g	50 g	60 ml
⅛	18 g	19 g	24 g	25 g	30 ml

Useful Equivalents for Liquid Ingredients by Volume

¼ tsp						=	1 ml	
½ tsp						=	2 ml	
1 tsp						=	5 ml	
3 tsp	=	1 Tbsp			=	½ fl oz	=	15 ml
		2 Tbsp	=	⅛ cup	=	1 fl oz	=	30 ml
		4 Tbsp	=	¼ cup	=	2 fl oz	=	60 ml
		5⅓ Tbsp	=	⅓ cup	=	3 fl oz	=	80 ml
		8 Tbsp	=	½ cup	=	4 fl oz	=	120 ml
		10⅔ Tbsp	=	⅔ cup	=	5 fl oz	=	160 ml
		12 Tbsp	=	¾ cup	=	6 fl oz	=	180 ml
		16 Tbsp	=	1 cup	=	8 fl oz	=	240 ml
		1 pt	=	2 cups	=	16 fl oz	=	480 ml
		1 qt	=	4 cups	=	32 fl oz	=	960 ml
						33 fl oz	=	1000 ml = 1 l

Useful Equivalents for Dry Ingredients by Weight

(To convert ounces to grams, multiply the number of ounces by 30.)

1 oz	=	⅟₁₆ lb	=	30 g
4 oz	=	¼ lb	=	120 g
8 oz	=	½ lb	=	240 g
12 oz	=	¾ lb	=	360 g
16 oz	=	1 lb	=	480 g

Useful Equivalents for Length

(To convert inches to centimeters, multiply the number of inches by 2.5.)

1 in					=	2.5 cm		
6 in	=	½ ft			=	15 cm		
12 in	=	1 ft			=	30 cm		
36 in	=	3 ft	=	1 yd	=	90 cm		
40 in					=	100 cm	=	1 m

Useful Equivalents for Cooking/Oven Temperatures

	Fahrenheit	Celsius	Gas Mark
Freeze water	32° F	0° C	
Room temperature	68° F	20° C	
Boil water	212° F	100° C	
Bake	325° F	160° C	3
	350° F	180° C	4
	375° F	190° C	5
	400° F	200° C	6
	425° F	220° C	7
	450° F	230° C	8
Broil			Grill

index